D1714413

About This Bool

A very interesting convergence and consensus which is now slowly emerging between the ancient sacred traditions and the most advanced thrusts of modern science is the emphasis that both give to an *alteration, transformation, and expansion of human consciousness.* This, they both assert, is truly fundamental for any presently adequate knowledge system and understanding of reality, whether objective—in the world, or subjective—within man. Both approaches recognize that, somehow, human consciousness, in its normal functioning, operates on three levels:

> The physical, or sensorial level.
> The emotional, or affective level.
> The mental, or cognitive level.

Both approaches also concur that, on these three levels, human consciousness is unable to penetrate to the core and true nature of reality, both in the microcosm—in man, and in the macrocosm—in the world. Thus, that a new and qualitatively different level of consciousness, i.e. "enlightened" or "spiritual" consciousness, is absolutely necessary for true science to continue its onward march into the nature of reality and for man to take his next evolutionary step in the present era; that this new level of consciousness needs deliberate and extended work on self to be achieved; and that, unlike the first levels, it is not a "free gift of nature" but, rather, a self-acquired fruit of art or labor.

The old religious injunction: "Seek ye first the Kingdom of Heaven (i.e. a new spiritual level of consciousness) and all these things shall be added unto you" (i.e. then you will be able to truly know yourself and your purpose on earth, and to understand reality) gets at the very heart of this matter in its own characteristic manner—which is to use appropriate symbolism or analogies.

One of the most fundamental questions for all earnest and serious seekers, and the very starting point of their true quest is, therefore: **How can I alter and expand my human consciousness so as to achieve at least some valid flashes of this new state of consciousness to guide me and inspire me in my quest?**

That's the question this book answers with the re-discovery and refinement of one's Spiritual Self, and the alignment of consciousness with it through the Seven Fundamentals of the Christian Tradition. Here is understanding of the traditional symbols and prayers of the church presented with effective exercises that achieve this goal—the accomplishment of which is the only true answer to the crisis of our times: that we may see our world with "new eyes".

About the Author

Born May 24, 1938 in Vevey, Switzerland, and educated in Switzerland, Argentina and Italy through secondary school, and in the United States, Germany and Canada at the University level. Graduated with honors from Columbia University, Phi Beta Kappa. Recipient of two Woodrow Wilson grants and received his Ph.D. from Fordham University in Sociology in 1972. In 1978, he received an MSW from the University of Montreal with a specialization in humanistic psychotherapy. He has studied with Pitirim Sorokin of Harvard University and was trained in Psychosynthesis by Roberto Assagioli of Florance, Italy.

He practices psychotherapy using personal and transpersonal Psychosynthesis with a particular interest in existential crisis due to psychic and spiritual awakening. For the last 15 years he has been teaching at East Stroudsburg University (Pennsylvania) where he is Professor of Sociology and Anthropology.

In 1980 he was knighted "Knight Commander of Malta". He is a member of the Board of Directors of the International Institute of Integral Human Studies of Montreal, Canada and Vice-President of the U.S. branch, and a past Field Faculty member of the Humanistic Psychology Institute of San Francisco. He is a Fellow of the American Orthopsychiatric Association, and is listed in most standard directories.

A productive writer, for the last 30 years, the *Leitmotif* of his life has been the study of spirituality and the investigation and development of spiritual consciousness. In these studies he has travelled widely to meet mystics, scholars, and spiritually awakened people who have provided him with "living models" for his investigations. He belongs to and holds high Offices in several esoteric and spiritual organizations, and considers this present work to embody the very best of his personal spiritual investigations and experiences.

To Write to the Author

We cannot guarantee that every letter written to the author can be answered, but all will be forwarded on to him. Both the author and the publisher appreciate hearing from readers, learning of your enjoyment and benefit from this book. Llewellyn also publishes a bi-monthly news magazine of New Age esoteric studies, and some readers' questions and comments may be answered through the *New Times'* columns if permission to do so is included in your original letter. The author participates in seminars and workshops, and dates and places may be announced in *The Llewellyn New Times*. To write to the author, or to secure a few sample copies of the *New Times,* write to:

Dr. Peter Roche de Coppens
c/o THE LLEWELLYN NEW TIMES
P.O. Box 64383-Dept. 675, St. Paul, MN 55164-0383, U.S.A.

Please enclose a self-addressed, stamped envelope for reply, or $1.00 to cover expenses.

About Llewellyn's Spiritual Perspective Series

SIMPLE, PRACTICAL, EFFECTIVE, COMPREHENSIVE, AUTHORITATIVE, INDIGENOUS TO OUR CULTURE

In a world and time that is becoming more complex, challenging and stressful, filled with "over choice" and "cognitive confusion", we are making available to you a unique series of books for self-exploration and growth that have the following distinctive features:

They are designed to be simple, cutting through abstraction, complexities and nuances that confuse and diffuse rather than enlighten and focus your understanding of your life's purpose.

They are practical; theory always leading to practice to be crowned by devotion when followed through by you as the experimenter. You are the ultimate "laboratory" and "judge".

They are effective, for if you do the work, you will obtain results of psychospiritual transformation and expansion of consciousness.

They are comprehensive because they integrate the exoteric with the esoteric, the sacred traditions of the past with the best insights of modern science.

They are authoritative because they are all written by persons who have actually lived and experienced what they tell you about.

They are part of our Western Culture and philosophical and Mystery Traditions, which must be understood if the synthesis of the Eastern and Western spiritual traditions and Universal Brotherhood is to be realized.

This series will reconcile the fragmented aspirations of ourselves, synthesize religion and science to bring about that psychosynthesis which is the greatest need of our age and its highest aspiration.

OTHER BOOKS FROM THE AUTHOR

Ideal Man in Classical Sociology,
   Pennsylvania State University Press, 1976
Spiritual Man in the Modern World,
   University Press of America, 1976
The Nautre and Use of Ritual,
   University Press of America, 1977, 1979
Spiritual Perspective,
   University Press of America, 1980
*Spiritual Perspectives II: The Spiritual Dimension and
   Implications of Love, Sex, and Marriage,*
      University Press of America, 1981

Forthcoming Titles from the author in the Llewellyn Spiritual Perspectives Series, which he was instrumental in creating, are:

The Nature and Use of Light and Power for Spiritual Attainment

The Challenges of our Times: Their Dangers and Opportunities

Llewellyn's Spiritual Perspectives Series

THE NATURE AND USE OF RITUAL FOR SPIRITUAL ATTAINMENT

By

Peter Roche de Coppens

1986
LLEWELLYN PUBLICATIONS
St. Paul, Minnesota, 55164-0383, U.S.A.

International Standard Book Number: 0-87542-675-1
Library of Congress Catalog Number: 85-10270

First Edition, 1985
First Printing, 1985
Second Printing, 1986

Library of Congress Cataloging in Publication Data

Roche de Coppens, Peter
  The nature and use of ritual for spiritual attainment.

  (Llewellyn's spiritual perspectives series)
  Rev. ed. of: The nature and use of ritual. Lanham, MD. : University Press of America, 1979.
  Bibliography: p.
  1. Spirituality—Christianity. 2. Man. 3. rutual.
I. Roche de Coppens, Peter. Nature and use of ritual.
II. Title. III. Series.
BV4501,2,R6174 1985   248,3   85-10270
ISBN 0-87542-675-1

**Cover Painting by Leslie Cohen Rogalski
Interior Illustrations by Bill Fugate
based on designs by author**

Produced by Llewellyn Publications
Typography and Art property of Chester-Kent, Inc.

Published by
LLEWELLYN PUBLICATIONS
A Division of Chester-Kent, Inc.
P.O. Box 64383
St. Paul, MN 55164-0383, U.S.A.

Printed in the United States of America

DEDICATION:
This work is dedicated to my beloved Teachers
Lydie, Theotokus, and Assagioli
and to my Brothers and Sisters in the Light
who have inspired and motivated this work
as well as to my students and readers,
known and unknown,
who are the "Living Laboratory"
for the Great Work.

TABLE OF CONTENTS

PREFACE

The Nature and Use of Ritual for Spiritual Attainment first came out under an abbreviated name in 1976 when it was published by the University Press of America*. The individual chapters which made up this work were written and rewritten between 1968 and 1974. At this time, each chapter was like a "seed" or a "thoughtform" which I planted in the "garden of my consciousness" and offered to students and friends for their own consideration and experimentation. Since then, each of these "seeds", which I first named the "Fundamentals of Universal Religion" has grown and born many fruits—in my own consciousness, life, and being, as in those of many other persons who experimented with them as well as in my writings and lectures.

For the last 10 years, I have applied, experimented with, and tested each of these "Fundamentals" in my own inner spiritual life, as well as my outer daily life in various lectures, workshops, and "personal and transpersonal growth groups" in the USA, Canada, and Europe.

I was very fortunate to be able to observe first-hand the results of this work in my own being and life, as well as that of

---

The Nature and Use of Ritual, University Press of America, 1979.

i

many others, and to get the enthusiastic feedback from many persons who had sought to integrate and live them in their own unique lives and being. Together we have given further "life, meaning, and depth" to these "Fundamentals", to embody and live its basic insights and teachings is, indeed, to "breathe life into it and enflesh them".

Were I to rewrite the basic chapters of this book today, I would probably add a few new ones as well as amplify with many lived examples and illustrations, and psychological, philosophical, and religious correspondences the existing ones. But the substance would remain the same, its essence would remain exactly what it is in the present edition for it is the present edition that is the "foundation" that gave life to all the rest!

When I was first meditating upon, then experimenting with and finally living in my own consciousness, these "Fundamentals", many times I felt as though an "invisible hand" was guiding my pen and opening my mind and understanding to an invisible Source I later named the "Western Spiritual Tradition".

This source of Life, Meaning, and Inspiration is far more alive and "real" to me today than it was at that time, for it has grown, enlarged its channels of communication and manifestation to me through the consciousness, words, writings, and lives of many other persons. Hence, today, it is for me both subjective and objective: a Living Tradition.

At the time when I first published this work, it represented the true quintessence of my spiritual search, experiences, and conclusions. Today, several years later, I still feel the same way, even though my overall perspective has broadened, and my practical experiences and realizations of the meaning, implications, and applications of these Seven Fundamentals have greatly expanded.

All of the basic insights and exercises contained in this

work have been diligently analyzed, studied, and "tested out" with the many practical spiritual groups I had formed as well as in my own being and life—which I took as the central "laboratory" to flesh out all the systems, ideas, and techniques I have ever come across. In fact, my understanding of these "Fundamentals" and my appreciation for what they can really do for the expansion of one's consciousness and one's spiritual growth have grown tremendously. They, themselves, have progressively unveiled and revealed to me, as I attempted to seriously live and embody them in my own life and to share them with others who also sought to incarnate these "mysteries", "treasures", and "possibilities" which I would hardly have suspected at the time!

The greatest "acid test" to which I, involuntarily, subjected them was to depend on their viability to keep me balanced, connected with the Inner Light, and aligned with my Higher Self during the most severe crisis and the greatest opportunity of my life where my very sanity and life were threatened and thus at stake.

It is because of the philosophy of life I developed, taught, and personally embodied, and of the theurgic insights and exercises contained in that work that I was able to obtain the proper understanding of my situation, and the intuitive insight I needed to make cognitive and affective sense of what was happening to me, and the *life, energies,* and *motivation* I needed to pull through it.

All the great Spiritual Traditions of the East and West bear in their own language and style the same basic message and fundamentals, and each focuses more specifically around certain aspects and facets that will unfold and manifest the soul and genius of the people it fashions and molds.

If this book is coming out today, it is because *it lives* and has become even more alive and vital than it was when it was first put together. My very life, consciousness, and writings have been touched, fashioned, and directed by its essence—for no one can teach for a long period of time that which one does not live.

Once you live what you contemplate and meditate upon in your quiet and silent hours, then it is the very thoughts and seeds one directs one's attention to that will unveil and reveal, progressively, their deeper meanings and living treasures, and one's understanding will then open to new dimensions and perspectives of one's self and of the world which would have otherwise remained hermetically sealed!

The actualization of potentialities, growth and unfoldment towards a greater consciousness, a life more abundant, and a wider freedom are indeed the great law of life . . . which explains why this work of mine has grown and is, again, being published.

The best definition I ever came across of the "New Age", its true nature and realization, was casually given to me by David Spangler when he stated:

"The New Age is not a new time or place but a *new state of consciousness,* the realization of which vitally depends on you and me . . . to transform our state of consciousness and level of being to personally achieve that new state of consciousness."

To bring about and enter into this "New Age" or "Promised Land", we need a viable Source of Revelation and Teachings that can get to the heart of our Being and of Reality; and a philosophy of life, an art of living, and a discipline that can be embodied, lived and realized by normal human beings, leading them to a gradual, organic and holistic (or "holy") transformation of their consciousness and being.

Every great World Religion and authentic metaphysical and philosophical system that recognizes the bio-psycho-spiritual nature of the Human Person and of Reality contains such a viable Source of Revelation and Guidance.

My basic aim in writing this work was to render explicit the essence or "Fundamentals" of the process of *bio-psycho-spiritual transformation* in terms of its core intuitions, its core instruments, progressive unfoldment, and basic proceedures, as it can be found in Christianity.

For the substance of this work comes from our own indigenous Spiritual Tradition; while it is unconsciously and mechanically paid "lip service" by millions of normal Christians, it constitutes the very heart of the process of bio-psycho-spiritual transformation, clothed in Western, Christian garb. Moreover, if one can find this Living Source of Revelation, Life and Inspiration in one tradition and realize it in one's consciousness, life, and being, then, but only then, can one also be able to find it in other traditions and finally reach that ultimate Planetary Synthesis of East and West, Male and Female, Old and New, Mind and Heart, and Science and Religion that will be the finest achievement of the coming age!

Reality and Life, both in Man (the microcosm) and in the World (the macrocosm) are, according to our deepest and finest thinkers and psychologists of the 20th century, structured and governed by *archetypes*. In a universe where "physics and metaphysics are the two aspects of the same reality", where "coincidence is really another name for Divine Providence", and where Life and its infinite manifestations are ruled by Universal Laws, all beings are necessarily the incarnation and embodiment of archetypes which structure and guide their unfolding and their destiny.

Man, who has rightly been called the microcosm or even Microtheos, who recapitualates all aspects of Creation and unites Heaven and Earth, must necessarily organize his life and growth in terms of Archetypes, symbols, myths and rituals. At least this is what the Sacred Scriptures of Humanity—Taoist, Buddhist, Vendantist, Judaic, Christian and Muslim—have asserted together with their great Saints and Sages.

But, as Carl Jung correctly pointed out: "The West has lost its myths" or, rather, the ability to comprehend and live the deeper meanings and implications of its sacred symbols, images, and rituals. Our sacred heritage is indeed immense and waiting out there for us to incorporate it in our lives and beings . . . but it must be properly deciphered, applied and incarnated.

Thus, one of the greatest and most authentic needs of our time is to learn anew how to decipher the sacred alphabets, to read the language of the Sages, and to interpret the Sacred Scriptures of the Spiritual Traditions . . . to make the great symbols, myths, and rituals of these traditions become alive and to "speak to us" in our consciousness and lives . . . And then we shall realize that the Truth and genuine Revelation have always been with us . . . even though official Religion, Science, and Philosophy may not have been aware of this!

This is precisely what the essence of this work attempts to do with very basic Christian Prayers and Documents—to reinterpret them in terms of their spiritual implications and practical applications, developing a model and showing the way to continue this process with all the great Spiritual Traditions and their sacred teachings and rituals.

The ultimate mystery is none other than of *Man Himself!* But it is not through the intellect that this mystery will ever be resolved; it is only through *Lived Experience* "apprehended" through the *Heart.*

"Know Thyself and thou shalt know the Universe and the Gods" claimed the Hermetic Wisdom. Thus we must know Man in the World and understand the World in Man as two sides of the same coin or reality.

The most fundamental question one can ask is: "How to help that which is 'below' find again the image or blue-print of that which is 'above', and the Path that leads to its realization". "Adam" is the 'Man from Below' and Elohim is the 'Man from above'.

To bring about this reconciliation, alignment, or attunement the living key is to rediscover and progressively enflesh the proper meaning, place, and function of the great symbols, myths, and rituals of our own consciousness and lives, for that is the Path of Wisdom! Moreover, to truly "Know Oneself" is to know *experientially* that, as Pascal put it: "There are two fundamental forms of knowing: that of the Head and that of the Heart, that of the Outer and that of the Inner Worlds as well as that of the Higher or Sacred Dimension and that of the Lower or Profane Dimension."

True knowledge or Wisdom is a marriage between the subject and the object, between the knower and the known; it is LOVE!

And this Path is the same Path that I have taken to decipher and live what I call the Seven Fundamentals . . . more cannot be said in words and must be *experienced in Silence* and *lived in one's own life* and this is where YOU the reader come in!

For the ultimate and living realization of these Treasures and Secrets of the Holy Wisdom now lie with YOU!

For the second edition of this fundamental work of mine, I would like to thank Carl Llewellyn Weschcke for giving flesh to my most compelling dream to publish a series of works on the Western Spiritual Tradition; Richard Urich for his simplification and 'Americanization' of the first version, and for the many hours he put into this "labor of love"; Aster Barnwell for his living example, support, and prayers; as well as many other friends, teachers, and students, who are too numerous to mention, who have provided me with ongoing support and inspiring feedback of this work with its most precious ingredient: unfolding human consciousness and developing potentials!

Chapter One

INTRODUCTION

Every age has what has aptly been called a *ZEITGEIST,* a spirit or ethos characterizing that age; an intellectual soul reflecting the central preoccupations, fears, experiences, and aspirations of the people who live, think, and work in it.

Every *Zeitgeist* has what are called "dominant themes" and "emergent themes." Dominant themes are those values and norms, those beliefs and aspirations which have been institutionalized by the culture at large and which are reflected in the consciousness, strivings, and daily lives of the majority. Emergent themes, on the other hand, are those new assumptions, ideals, and aspirations which are proposed and espoused by a creative minority. This creative and "evolutionary" minority, dissatisfied with the current realities and opportunities offered by their society, are seeking and laboring for something that is "higher" and more genuinely satisfying than what they can find in the world in which they are living.

The dominant themes of our age are the questions of national and international peace, of social justice or injustice, of social reform or revolution, of material success and affluence, of science, secular humanism, and global industrial-

1

ism.

The most dynamic emergent themes of our epoch are those dealing with an ecology of the Earth, of the psyche, and of the spirit; the question of the meaning and purpose of man, life, and the universe; of human growth and self-expression; of personal and collective self-actualization and Self-realization.

These dominant and emergent themes are essentially the old but perennial spiritual quest in modern dress and form: that we are unfinished animals summoned to unfold astonishing possibilities, to further unfold our human consciousness and to actualize our human and spiritual faculties.

Having explored and conquered the outer physical world, harnessed the raw materials and the physical energies of nature through science and technology, and developed an urban and industrial civilization which now reigns supreme in most advanced nations, but having failed to find either a lasting inner or outer peace, satisfying justice or goodness, true beauty or genuine purpose, an ever greater number of people are now turning, in their unending and ever-renewed search for happiness, toward an exploration of the inner worlds of the psyche, towards the latent energies and faculties of the mind, and towards the unexplored heights and potentialities of the spirit.

To an outer and physical science and technology of the material universe, and to an extroverted preoccupation with nature and a higher standard of living, we must now slowly and painfully develop an inner and psychic "science" and "technology" of the human psyche, an introverted investigation of man himself and his meaning, purpose, and destiny.

The truly fundamental and universal questions that have always faced man and that will always confront him, especially when he slowly awakens from his mental amnesia, from his emotional narcosis, and from his spiritual slumber, are no more answered today than they were a few centuries ago before the beginning of the modern age. In fact, because of the slow decay of those social institutions which provided ready-made answers to these questions, they are perhaps even less satisfactorily answered today than they were a few centuries ago.

Yet man's present psychological stirrings and conflicts, and his existential dilemmas and trials are now pressing down upon him, perhaps more acutely than before, to find or fashion viable answers to them or to perish both psychologically and socially. The need to find it is desperate; it is possibly the central need of our times and so many people, each in his own way, are responding to it.

Briefly put, the great questions for mankind are:

A. THE RIDDLE OF THE SPHINX: What is man? What am I? Where do I come from? What am I supposed to do here? Why am I here on Earth? How should I live?

B. THE ENIGMA OF LIFE: What is life? Where does it come from and where is it going? What is its purpose and how do I fit in that purpose?

C. THE PUZZLE OF THE UNIVERSE: What is the universe? Where does it come from and where is it going? Who or what created it and for what purpose? And how do I fit in this purpose?

Ever since the Renaissance, and particularly the Age of Enlightenment, philosophy and science have pointed to the physical universe, and external nature, as being the guardian of the ultimate answer to these questions and have suggested that objective observation, logical reasoning, and much experimentation would ultimately provide meaningful and satisfying answers. But, alas, they have not!

The great promise of the Renaissance and of the Enlightenment has not been realized; the logico-experimental method of this age has not provided deeper meanings, larger synthesis, and a life more abundant for larger numbers of people. All it has produced is more material affluence for some and more dehumanized misery for others, much greater power and physical energies but much less wisdom and goodness to use these powers and energies constructively. Thus the creative potential and the exploration of this cultural approach are now nearly exhausted, with the substantial answers nowhere in sight, while our material resources have been ruthlessly exploited and depleted, and human conflicts have reached the point where a major conflagration could easily explode, destroying our sanity and our civiliztion.

It is not only understandable but also imperative that many people, particularly the young, the most concerned, the most sensitive, and the brightest should now turn towards the inner space, looking within themselves through introspection and meditation, in the desperate hope to wrest from the depths and the heights of their own being those long-sought and repressed answers which have become so crucial for our very own physical, let alone psychological, survival. Thus the foundations of our culture are again changing and we are witnessing both the "death" of an old world and the "birth" of a new world.

The "rediscovery" and exploration of the inner spaces, of the latent energies and faculties of the psyche, and of the dormant potentialities and powers of the spirit have produced a wide variety of results and approaches.

Very different types of persons and groups were drawn to this quest by very different motives; on the one hand we have the established religions with their ancient traditions, their symbols, rituals, and ceremonies which are repositories of the HIDDEN WISDOM and of the MYSTERIES, but which have lost, for the most part, their ancient mystical and practical explanations and applications that were based in an ORAL TRADITION. Thus they have failed to develop a practical interpretation of their tradition that fits the needs and the consciousness of our age. Precious treasures of the Hidden Wisdom can, indeed, be found there but, alas, not their meaningful explanation or integrated practical exercises.

What organized religions have is a BODY and a SPIRIT of the sacred traditions; what they lack is a SOUL: a practical and meaningful interpretation that can be accepted and used by the educated members of our society and by our searching youth who need high ideals and a sound discipline so badly.

On the other hand, we have parapsychological and extrasensory research using the methods and approaches of the natural sciences. Consequently, this approach is getting lost in a maze of statistics and tests which may, indeed, be sensational and startling, but which totally lacks the essence and the spirit of what is being investigated. Both subjects and researchers are generally psychodynamically and spiritually untrained, and indescriminately selected, lacking the discipline and the frame of reference necessary to be truly productive in this field.

Finally, we have guardians of ancient and not so ancient esoteric traditions who veil their insights and teachings behind a nearly impenetrable and, many times, outdated language and symbolism, and who keep whatever truth and techniques they have by impressive but largely sterile oaths of silence within the walls of their temples. And we also have the "freaks" and other "drop outs" of the "consciousness circuit" who travel from center to center, from guru to guru, and from one tradition or fad to another.

The genuine esoteric orders *do exist,* to be sure, but they do not advertise and their members, who use a great deal of discretion and a good dose of common sense, can only be recognized, here and there, by their vital and dynamic personalities, their kindness and penetrating wisdom, and the many people they have and are helping.

In this jungle of confusion, this quicksand of counterfeit

and instant wisdom, where can the earnest and sincere seeker turn? This is a truly fundamental question which I have asked myself for many years and which has guided me through many adventures, and even more misadventures, in the labyrinth of the occult circuit. The carefully weighted answers I would give to this question, drawn from my own personal experiences, trials, and errors, is:

First and foremost the devotee should turn to himself and his own personal growth and development, purification and consecration. He should acquire systematic self-knowledge, then self-mastery, and finally Self-realization. There is simply no substitute for these "simple fundamentals" and they *must be acquired,* however painfully and slowly, through some form of humanistic therapy or psychosynthesis.

This is all the more important in an age, such as ours, when external authorities of all sorts are slowly disintegrating and contradicting each other. Our age is truly the age in which earnest and mature seekers are compelled to turn inwards, to undertake the "inward journey to their source," to seek refuge in the "Inner Fortress," and guidance from the Inner Light.

Second, the seeker should turn to the sacred traditions of the past as embodied by the great World Religions, on the one hand, and to the valid Mystery Schools or Esoteric Orders, on the other—for both mutually complement and reinforce each other.

Third, the devotee should turn to the guidance and the living example of another human being who has proven his "wisdom" by what he *is,* by how he *lives,* and by what he *does* rather than merely by what he *says* or *preaches.*

Fourth, he should turn to the best of modern science and integrate what he can learn here with the Mysteries in a creative and vivifying synthesis; for science is slowly but surely advancing towards the discovery of the inner spaces, the latent powers of the mind, and the realization of the spiritual realms and energies.

Science, here, should be understood as the method of direct, personal observation and experience as opposed to the method of relying on the words, discoveries, and experiences of others.

This new approach is very important and constitutes a distinctive feature of the New Age: ancient revelation, wisdom, and spiritual teachings must now be expressed in a "scientific form," i.e., the spirit of the Ageless Wisdom must be provided with a new "form," the form corresponding to our age which, being essentially a mental age, can best be expressed in "scientific" language.

The word "science" should be defined in the sense in which I am using it; otherwise it could lead to further confusion and controversy. To me this word means basically two things:

1. An objective, systematic, and precise study of any area or aspect of reality, whether in the microcosm or in the macrocosm, which is grounded in either direct observation or in direct experience. The recognition of the difference between observation and experience is crucial for there are many aspects of reality (e.g. ideas, emotions, states of consciousness, love, and enlightenment) which unlike material things or behavior, cannot be seen but which can be experienced. Thus, while the natural sciences deal more with the observable part of the "empirical world"* the human and social sciences deal more with the humanly experienced side of the same empirical world.

2. It also implies working with the method developed

---

*EMPIRICAL WORLD: Those facets of the world which are open to direct observation and experience.

by Frances Bacon which many of our modern, dogmatic, and close-minded "sciences" have largely departed from, falling into new "metaphysics," "delusions," and finally even "superstitions" (e.g. materialism, positivism, and behaviorism). Simply put, the method advocated by Bacon operates in such a way as to clear or purify the mind from many conscious or unconscious "idols," or distortions which involuntarily clutter and distort its perceptions and conclusions. Bacon listed four major "idols" which, unfortunately, are still very much with us today and which distort the views of laymen and scientists alike, namely:

Idols of the cave which he defined as "prejudices due to the nature of the individual," i.e. unconscious and subconscious drives and impulses originating in our biopsychic nature and in our character.

Idols of the tribe which he defined as "prejudices due to the customs of the human race," i.e. influences and impulses originating in the collective unconscious and subconscious, and in the character of our sociocultural milieu which, subliminally, affects man's mind and perceptions.

Idols of the market place which he defined as "prejudices due to the use of words," i.e. semantical distortions and social definitions which slant or distort the true nature of certain words and symbols, confusing or mixing-up the three different languages of every day speech, science and religion.

Idols of the theater which he defined as "prejudices due to the influence of great names," i.e. the compelling and sometimes distorting influence of established "authorities."

These idols, or distortions, Bacon claimed, should be replaced by direct and precise observations, experiments and analysis.

Both science and the sacred traditions emphasize an

alteration, transformation, and expansion of human consciousness. Both approaches recognize that somehow, a normal functioning human consciousness operates on three levels, namely:

    THE PHYSICAL or sensorial level,
    THE EMOTIONAL or affective level,
    THE MENTAL or cognitive level.

On these three levels, human consciousness is unable to penetrate to the core and true nature of reality, both in the microcosm in man, and the macrocosm—the world. Thus, a new and qualitatively different level of consciousness (enlightened or spiritual consciousness) is absolutely necessary for true science to continue its onward march into the nature of reality and for man to take his next evolutionary step in the present era; that this new level of consciousness needs deliberate and extended work on itself to be achieved; and unlike the first levels, it is not a free gift of nature, but rather, a self-acquired fruit of art or labor.

The old religious injunction: "SEEK YE FIRST THE KINGDOM OF HEAVEN (i.e. a new spiritual level of consciousness) AND ALL THESE THINGS SHALL BE ADDED UNTO YOU" (i.e. then you will truly know yourself, your purpose on Earth, and to understand reality) gets at the very heart of this matter in its own characteristic manner, which is to use appropriate symbolism or analogies.

One of the most fundamental questions for all earnest and serious seekers, and the very starting point of their true quest is:

> How can I alter and expand my human consciousness so as to achieve at least some valid flashes of this new state of consciousness to guide me and inspire me in my quest?

While there are many routes and approaches that lead to different altered and expanded states of consciousness, in all of these we can recognize and select certain basic elements which are:

Obtaining the proper knowledge of the effective means to do so in a safe and balanced way.

Unfolding the motivation and the energies to apply effectively these means and to carry out the work required.

Developing the right motives and judgment for doing so and then using in a positive and constructive manner the new energies and faculties which will be forthcoming.

The answer given to this great quest for "rebirth" (i.e. an effective transformation and expansion of consciousness) by the sacred traditions and now increasingly more the humanistic, transpersonal and height* schools of modern psychology, *is the fusion and synthesis of worship* (the love of God) *with service* (the love of man).

Around these are also grounded the twin aims of *self-actualization:* psychosocial work aiming at the development of the personality, and *Self-realization:* psychospiritual work aiming at discovering one's spiritual Self and aligning one's consciousness with It. Whatever approach or system is used, these are the "basic fundamentals" which must be confronted and slowly acquired and internalized.

Worship, in its inner structure, contains a "male" and a "female" polarity, the first being RITUAL and its proper use, while the second is SILENCE and its proper achievement.

Service, too, includes a "male" and a "female" polarity: actively helping others to effectively enhance their being and lives and allowing them to help and enrich themselves.

The present study will focus mainly upon Ritual and its

---

*Modern schools of psychology have been subdivided into three distinct groups: the first is the so-called "depth-psychology" school which gives great importance to the unconscious and to exploring and cleaning up the "depths" of such unconscious. Psychoanalysis and the Neo-Freudian approaches are the best examples of "depth psychology". Then, we have the "surface" or "behavioral psychologies" that focus upon behavior in the "here and now" and that by-pass the unconscious. Behaviorism and Neo-Behaviorism are the best examples of this school. The "Third force" and the last movement to appear in modern psychology is the so-called "height psychology" school which recognizes and gives great importance not only to the lower unconscious, but to the higher unconscious, or superconscious, as well. Humanistic psychology, transpersonal psychology, and psychosynthesis are examples of contemporary "height psychology".

proper use at the theoretical level, and its specific development and application in the "Seven Fundamentals of the Christian Tradition" although these may equally well be applied to other "Fundamentals" of other religious traditions.

It is the ritualistic use of these seven fundamentals—which contain a true "science" and "art" of human and spiritual development—that both the necessary knowledge and the proper motivation, and the correct motives and judgement can be found and slowly unfolded through specific practical exercises.

Each of these fundamentals contains symbols, glyphs, and practical exercises which are designed to set in motion the "intuitive faculty," to bring about a genuine breakthrough of the superconscious into the conscious, and to lead to the dawning of spiritual consciousness.

Each demands the proper use and development of specific functions of the psyche through its appropriate process, leads to the psychological preparation necessary for the inrush of new energies, and brings as its byproduct an emergent knowledge and understanding which will guide the seeker in his spiritual adventure.

These psychospiritual "calesthenics," are *not a substitute* for a clean, constructive, and balanced life which should precede and accompany them. This is clearly and explicitly pointed out by one of the oldest spiritual systems known to mankind, the YOGA SUTRAS of Patanjali. Here seven steps or stages are developed: Yama-Niyama, Asana, Prana-yama, Pratyahara, Dharana, Dhyana, Samadhi. Yama-Niyama, are the basic "do's" and "do nots," or an ethical attitude and practice towards which should precede all later phases. Asana and Pranayama are the physical training and breathing exercises leading to a balanced life. Pratyahara, Dharana, and Dhyana are respectively Concentration, Meditation, and Contemplation. Samadhi is spiritual Illumination or Union with God, the final phase of the whole system.

Our investigation of Ritual and its proper use deals specifically with Concentration, Meditation, and Contemplation leading eventually to Union with God. All too often, unfortunately, contemporary seekers forget or by-pass the Yama-Niyama (do's and don'ts) stage, and sometimes the Asana-Niyama (physical training and breathing exercises) phase with very deleterious effects for their emotional and mental health and for their human relationships.

THESE STAGES ARE THE *SINE QUA NON* FOR THE MATURE SEEKER AND CANNOT BE NEGLECTED OR BY-PASSED WITHOUT REAPING SEVERE CONSEQUENCES.

YOGA SUTRAS OF PANTANJALI

1. YAMA-NIYAMA.................... DO'S AND DON'TS OF LIFE
2. ASANA.................................. PHYSICAL TRAINING
3. PRANAYAMA......................... BREATHING EXERCISES
4. PRATYAHARA .... CONCENTRATION
5. DHARAMA....................................... MEDITATION
6. DHYANA.................................... CONTEMPLATION
7. SAMADHI..................... SPIRITUAL ILLUMINATION and UNION WITH GOD

In the conscious and proper use of Ritual, the will is developed through the process of *concentration,* i.e. focusing one's whole attention and awareness upon a chosen subject or point at the exclusion of all other things, or turning one's mind into a "magnifying glass," and later through the process of *affirmation.*

Thinking is developed through the process of *meditation* bringing in its wake much additional knowledge by way of new associations, correspondences, and relationships.

Feeling is developed through the process of *devotion* and *adoration,* i.e. exalting and purifying one's emotions by focusing them devotionally upon the Divine within.

Finally imagination is developed through the process of

visualization, which again focuses upon the Divine within with images and archetypes that act as psychic channels of expression.

As the symbols, petitions, and the whole glyph of the given fundamental is deciphered in terms of its various meanings, correspondences, and implications on various "planes" or states of consciousness and as the various practical exercises it contains are revealed and properly understood and applied, then comes the final phase—its *theurgic use* in *invocation* and *evocation* through which human aspiration is answered by spiritual inspiration, and the breakthrough between the superconscious and conscious is established and realized through experience!

Practically speaking, the proper procedure is to:

1. Write down the chosen fundamental and break it down in terms of its component parts, i.e. its symbols.

2. Develop the will and the power of concentration by first concentrating on one symbol, then on one petition, and finally on the whole document.

3. Develop thinking and meditation by meditating first on one symbol, then on one petition, and finally on the whole document to decipher its inner meanings, correspondences, and practical applications. Each new meaning *should then be filed away in the subconscious memory for later use.*

4. Amplify and exalt feeling and "make prayer come alive" by directing all your love and emotions first on one symbol, then on one petition, and finally on the whole document, to progressively generate and express greater love for the Divine Within and the Great Work.

5. Train and cultivate imagination and visualization by visualizing (and letting new images and symbols flow before your mental "screen" of vision) first one symbol, then one petition, and finally the whole

document.

6. File away, in your workbook and in your mind, all the practical implications and exercises discovered thus far.

7. Finally, use one symbol, one petition, or the whole document to practice one and then the other exercises that have been "revealed" by bringing together concentration, meditation, devotion, and visualization into an upward-thrusting *invocation;* wait for an answer, a response, an awakening, or the ensuing *evocation.* After this has occurred, RECORD THE EVENT and the experience you just went through in your workbook.

The practical exercises, the invocations and its following evocations can be used for one's self as well as for others, for specific as for general purposes, to awaken a given psycho-spiritual center or the whole Tree of Life.*

Their applications are practically limitless and deepen as one continues with the work and achieves more advanced stages. The faculties, powers, and new states of consciousness thus trained and unfolded can be used for worship as well as for service, for spiritual as well as psychological development, for sacred as well as for "profane" purposes.

Engaged in long enough and with enough persistence, they will gradually lead to the development of a new personality and of a new life, permeating and affecting all of one's inter-personal relationships and activities.

Integrated with the other aspects of the Great Work, with "LIVING THE LIFE," with a proper and personal

---

*According to both the Eastern and the Western Spiritual Traditions, the anatomy and physiology of the subtle bodies of human beings (the etheric, astral, mental, and spiritual bodies) contain centers of Light and Energy that are intimately connected with one's state of consciousness. In the East, these centers are, generally, connected with the etheric body. They are 7 in number, and they are called "Chakras" or "Wheels". In the West, these centers are, generally, connected with the astral, mental, and spiritual bodies. They are 10 in number though only 7 can be activated while a human being is incarnate, and they are called "Sephiroth" or "Roses". For further information on these centers and their distribution in the Tree of Life, see Appendix D.

rhythm of PRAYER, WORK, and RELAXATION, and with constructive activities and a rich and satisfying social life, this training will eventually lead one to true Samadhi—to spiritual Illumination or "Union with God" which is the greatest and ultimate purpose of life on Earth and man's true destiny.

The core of this book and the following chapters are made up of a series of integrated lectures which I gave at different times and places, and finally as an interrelated Seminar on the topics of Worship, Ritual, and the Seven Fundamentals. Thus each chapter is both an autonomous unit and a sequential step in an organic process. Each contains a theoretical development as well as practical applications of Ritual, its nature, uses, and possibilities. Each embodies vital principles, exercises, and actual psycho-spiritual "calesthenics" which, taken together, form a complete curriculum in human and spiritual development.

Let the reader keep in mind at all times that it is up to him to do the required work, to train his faculties, psychological functions and to progressively unveil the various meanings, correspondences, and associations, these "fundamentals" contain, and to discover their practical applications.

The work of the interpretation and deciphering of these fundamentals and sets of symbols is merely the beginning of a long path; it is not a substitute for the reader's own meditations and work; it is merely a simple and practical example of what can and should be done, of how this work can be carried out, and of the great rewards and self-growth it can bring.

Chapter Two

THE GREAT WORK: ITS NATURE, ESSENCE, AND REALIZATION

Ever since man unfolded the power of thinking, of reflecting upon the nature of life, of the universe, and of himself, he has consciously or unconsciously become involved with the Great Work.

In all places where human culture developed and at all times, the more serious and concerned thinkers have become interested in and begun to work upon what came to be known as the Great Work or MAGNUM OPUS.

At the core of what has been called the Ancient or Ageless Wisdom, we can find the Great Work, just as we can find it in the heart of true religion and philosophy, for it is indeed the most important and highest human achievement. Countless books, essays, and elucidations of the Great Work have been offered by different traditions, schools, and organizations.

In this chapter we will attempt to get at the substance of the Great Work and to describe it in as simple and practical terms as possible as to its nature, essence, and purpose and how it can be realized by individuals who are earnest seekers aspiring to more in life than what their culture and the example of their fellow men offers.

In all religious, metaphysical, philosophical, and even esoteric traditions, we find that the Great Work, in its essence, has always stood for three basic endeavors:

THE STUDY OF MAN
MAN'S CONSCIOUS IMPROVEMENT
THE REALIZATION OF MAN'S ULTIMATE PERFECTION

This is the true heart and core of the Great Work whatever its manifold external expressions, aspects, and degrees may be.

At the foundation of the Great Work we find the three great Greek injunctions:

MAN, KNOW THYSELF!
MAN, BECOME THE MASTER OF THYSELF
MAN, SEEK UNION WITH THYSELF; BECOME THY HIGHER SELF!

From the foregoing it is clear that the Great Work really deals with the most important and highest task that any mature human being can engage in; and that it deals with the very essence of what man has come to Earth to accomplish.

The chief aim of the Great Work can also be found in the short explanation that Jesus (as all true spiritual Teachers of humanity) has given to His life and work: "I have come that you may have a life more abundant." If there is one thing that is sacred in this world and which can be immediately be recognized as such, it is LIFE; for it is life with its essence and all of its attributes that is the most important or "holy thing." If we accept this statement then it becomes apparent that man's greatest task is to consciously expand, heighten, and deepen the expression of LIFE, in all its manifestations; both in himself and in others.

To "consciously expand, heighten and deepen the expression of life" implies, first and foremost, to know what life is, to be able to recognize and identify the manifold manifestations of life within and around oneself, and to be able to experience the unfoldment of life in one's daily existence. Thus the Great Work begins with a systematic work on oneself, whatever the discipline and tradition used to accomplish this may be.

Both in the world and in man, life has three fundamental expressions:

THE PHYSICAL
THE PSYCHIC
THE SPIRITUAL

While these three expressions are both qualitatively and quantitatively different from one another, each obeying its own distinctive laws, in essence they are one as life is fundamentally one. This, incidentally, is one of the mysteries and major applications of the Trinity which plays such an important role in the Western Spiritual Tradition.

On the physical level life manifests itself essentially as growth and change; on the psychic planes as consciousness; and on the spiritual planes as the source and substance of life or LIGHT.

In creation, life descends from the Divine Plane to the Physical Plane in successive phases of involution that imprison and restrict life in more and more material forms. Having reached its "nadir of crystallization" in matter, life then begins to reascend the Planes back to its Divine Source and Origin through successive phases of evolution. Here life manifests through different "vehicles" that become more and more differentiated and sensitive as time goes by and expresses and unfolds itself essentially as consciousness; which allow for an increasingly more conscious expression of life.

Man here can be seen as the most advanced and complex set of vehicles for the expression of life from the Physical to the Divine Planes. But man is not yet a finished being; he is an incomplete being undergoing an evolution, the aim of which is to perfect and complete his being. Thus, in man, life and human consciousness are, therefore, the essential essence of man.

The history of man on Earth is the biography of the progressive unfoldment of human consciousness from its animal origins to its spiritual destiny.

In man, nature becomes conscious of itself and God finds a conscious vehicle of expression in creation.*

The achievement of self-knowledge, therefore, involves the systematic study of human consciousness, its structures and functions, and its conscious and active expansion. The history of human civilization and culture, the countless vicissitudes of man on Earth are but an unconscious way of unfolding his human consciousness, both horizontally and vertically through many planes of being.

Traditionally, theology tackled this problem from one angle and science from another angle, with philosophy seeking to synthesize the two from its own perspective. Today, however, these basic branches of human knowledge have splintered into the various "natural sciences", "social sciences", an anemic "theology" which has lost most of its erstwhile prestige and authority, and a philosophy that has done all but foresake its traditional synthesizing function for all knowledge.

The need for *Illumination*† and for *Holiness*‡ have remained as constant, perennial, and unfulfilled needs of man, assuming different forms and manifestations at different periods in his history and cultural development. Since the last great revolution of consciousness and knowledge which took place during the 19th century, and which focused upon a rational view of reality and synthesis of knowledge, man has sought self-knowledge, self-mastery, and self-actualization

---

*Expressed in the symbols of the *Hagia Sophia,* life which is "force" in the "Father" and "form" in the "Mother", unfolds as "consciousness" in the "Son".

†ILLUMINATION: Development of the faculties and abilities necessary for obtaining and synthesizing an integral knowledge of reality, both in its outer and inner aspects.

‡HOLINESS: Development and unification at the conscious level of one's whole being.

evermore desperately but fruitlessly as he proceeded in a direction where these could not be found. From the second half of the 19th century to the end of the first half of the 20th century, the sacred traditions of the past surfaced again in various mystical, occult, magical, and spiritual "schools" and "disciplines" characterized by a strong esoteric flavor and orientation. These were clearly counter-cultural and deviant in their basic assumptions and conclusions, and especially in their methods of presentation; thus, they were rejected by the scientific, academic, and theological ortho- doxies which ridiculed them, surrounded them by a wall of silence or sensationalism, and dismissed them as heresies and superstitions of the past.

However, these schools and disciplines contained the "missing links" and the synthesis which our anemic theology and our ever splintering sciences had lost and were searching for, in vain, in the wrong direction and through inappropriate methodolgies.

Culture and counter-culture will eventually have to be synthesized at a higher level, containing the essence and best of what is valid for both; this is what we see happening today and to which we should all hope to make some modest contribution.

Religion, philosophy, and science were once unified and integrated in a harmonious whole which constitutes the true science and art of the sacred traditions; their central aim being the production of true sages or Priest-Philosopher- Kings.

Today the same need and ideal is surfacing again. The thrust, which is more or less conscious and deliberate in various thinkers and searchers, is to produce a synthesis of the best of modern human and social sciences with the valid insights of the great sacred traditions of the past, and to fuse religious and esoteric disciplines with the methodologies and insights of modern psychology to generate a higher form of therapy which will operate as a functional substitute for the

Mysteries of the past.

Here, the new sanity and ideal which is now being envisioned is not only to heal those who are sick, and to help the maladapted person adjust to his social environment and learn how to "live with himself," but also and especially to actualize his latent potentialities and faculties, to transcend himself and thus fulfill his true destiny.

In the past, self-knowledge, self-mastery, and self-actualization were high and distant goals reserved for the few who where set apart from the rest of humanity and who were especially trained for this purpose through rigorous and very demanding disciplines. Today, these great and fundamental aims of human nature are open to all who truly search for and desire them, and can be realized through methodologies which are designed to get down to the essentials of the work, cutting out all the details and the unnecessary ideological and semantical adornments and encumbrances with which they were clothed and masked in the past. The Quest and its essentials remain the same but its cultural vehicles and expressions must be adapted to our present times and needs. Thus the Great Work is, once again, reappearing on the contemporary scene, clothed in modern dress and carried out through a modern approach which answers the needs, ideals, and consciousness of our age.

At the heart of the Great Work we find certain very simple, universal, and unchanging elements which can be summarized as follows:

1. A psychospiritual discipline aiming at consciously altering, transforming, and expanding human consciousness so as to give birth to a new and qualitatively different type of consciousness — SPIRITUAL CONSCIOUSNESS!

2. A philosophy of life and an ethic by which to organize and structure one's entire daily life so as to progressively incarnate and live what was revealed in

the higher state of consciousness.

This psychospiritual discipline and way of life are grounded in the two central axes of all genuine traditions, i.e. the love of God and the love of man. In the Western Spiritual Tradition, the specific formulation of these two main axes is: "Thou shalt love the Lord thy God, with all thy heart, with all thy soul, and all thy mind, and thy fellow man as thyself."

Underpinning the love of God is WORSHIP, climbing the sacred Mountain wherein the Divine dwells and can be encountered.

Underpinning the love of man is SERVICE, helping one's fellow men to unfold their being and actualize their potentialities to the highest extent so that life may express through them as consciously and as fully as possible.

The science (knowledge) and art (practice) of effective worship and the science and art of effective service constitute

---

WORSHIP
THE MALE or ACTIVE ASPECT
RITUAL or THEURGY
1. CONCENTRATION
2. MEDITATION
3. DEVOTION
4. VISUALIZATION

PROCEDURE: Systematically raise the Life Force and Psychic Voltage

THE FEMALE or PASSIVE ASPECT
ENTERING THE SILENCE

	MALE POLARITY
1. PHYSICAL WORLD	··················
	FEMALE POLARITY
	MALE POLARITY
2. EMOTIONAL WORLD	··················
	FEMALE POLARITY
	MALE POLARITY
3. MENTAL WORLD	··················
	FEMALE POLARITY
	FEMALE POLARITY
4. SPIRITUAL WORLD	··················
	MALE POLARITY

PROCEDURE: Systematically increase receptivity and sensitivity

---

the very center of the spiritual life which was and is the aim of the sacred traditions. Moreover, worship must precede service for in order to have the means to truly help one's fellow-man, one must be illuminated, vitalized, and guided by the light of the Spirit.

The synthesis and culmination of worship and service is union with God (or with one's spiritual Self) which has ever been the final and supreme goal of the sacred traditions.

The modern social sciences which are now aiming at developing a "science of man", an effective art of living, and a comprehensive philosophy of life with a practical ethic, are aiming in exactly the same direction.

Beginning with direct experience rather than with "conceptualized revelation", and starting with the known and the conscious to thrust towards the unknown and the superconscious, they are also aiming at an effective form of worship, psychospiritual development, and a practical art of living, or right human relationships.

Under different names and preceding through different methodologies, the Path and the Quest are one and the same. Thus in Psychosynthesis (which is the most advanced form and the best synthesis of the modern social sciences) the Great Work is developed through the following stages:

1. Acquiring a systematic knowledge of:
    The Field of Consciousness and the seven functions of the Psyche—willing, thinking, feeling, intuition, imagination, biopsychic drives, and sensations.
    The Subconscious—the stored memories of one's entire life and the way to get at them and organize them.
    The Unconscious—the biopsychic drives, instincts, and complexes, and a way to integrate them.
    The Superconsious—the creative spiritual energies and materials of the higher Self and of Its sphere of consciousness, and how to bring them down and

integrate them in the psyche.

2. Acquiring mastery of:
   The functions of the psyche and their coordination.
   The materials of the subconscious.
   The energies and materials of the unconscious.
   The energies, inspirations, and materials of the super-conscious.

3. Discovering one's human and spiritual Self and aligning one's personality with them.

4. Creating a new and this time consciously fashioned personality as the trained vehicle for the human and spiritual Self.

Beginning with a "Personal Psychosynthesis" which deals with the systematic exploration and organization of one's own psyche, this approach then leads to an "Inter-personal Psychosynthesis" wherein one interacts with others, and discovering one's own "psychological types" and how to meaningfully relate to them.

Both stages culminate in *Self-Actualization* which is the conscious development and organization of one's person-ality. Self-actualization then leads to the third stage, trans-personal or *Spiritual Psychosynthesis,* which consists in discovering and aligning one's human self and personality with the spiritual Self, which culminates in *Self-Realization,* the offering of a *trained* and *efficient* TEMPLE, or vehicle, to the Spirit for the manifestation of its attributes in the world.

Without the building of the "TEMPLE OF SOLOMON" (i.e. the self-actualized personality), the Life, Light, and Fire of the Spirit would have no way of becoming conscious of themselves in the world, and of manifesting themselves therein.

Without the Quest for God, the discovery of the spiritual Self, or Self-realization, the most perfectly developed personality would have neither an ultimate purpose nor a true source of life and being; thus both must work together.

In dealing with an effective science and art of worship, which is crucial both to the sacred traditions of the past and to modern psychosynthesis, the synthesis of these two has come up with a very useful and practical scheme: Clarify which functions of the psyche are used, through what processes, and with what results in the practice of worship, and train these faculties so that they can be used effectively. Thus:

1. WILLING is used in concentration and affirmation which provides energy and a focus to the whole operation.

2. THINKING is used in meditation in its threefold stages of reflective, receptive, and contemplative meditation. This provides knowledge and the focusing of the mind.

3. FEELING is used in adoration or devotion which provides energy, emotion, and drive.

4. IMAGINATION is used in visualization, which can become vision when fired by the spiritual energies, and provides life, focus, and motivation.

5. INTUITION is obtained through the creative fusion of aspiration operating through invocation and of inspiration operating through evocation (or through the synthesis of human effort and Divine Grace). From this synthesis results an actual breakthrough of the Superconscious into the conscious, which is the central objective of both the sacred traditions and transpersonal psychology.

6. BIOPSYCHIC DRIVES, impulses and desires, can and should be harnessed and their powerful energies channelled and focused through self-mastery and transmutation.

7. SENSATIONS can be developed and amplified through careful and precise observation and sensory awareness exercises.

The dawning of a new and qualitatively different stage of consciousness—Spiritual consciousness—is the first great goal of all human disciplines which are answering the deepest and truest needs of our age and which provides the foundation for the beginning, as well as the completion, of the Great Work of man in its universal form of a genuine psychosynthesis, a working social integration, and an experienced union with God.

Chapter Three

SPIRITUALITY AND THE SPIRITUAL TRADITION

What is Spirituality?

Briefly put, spirituality is the "fruit" and the ultimate end of all religions, Christian and non-Christian, Western and Eastern, primitive and modern, which they seek to achieve and to foster in their devotees. It is also the evolutionary stage in human development which we call 'maturity" and the state of being and consciousness which all human beings are, consciously or unconsciously, striving to achieve. It is the goal of human evolution and the destiny of man towards which all human experiences and all human endeavors are leading.

Spirituality is essentially a state of human consciousness—a certain way of thinking, feeling, and willing which profoundly affects our way and style of living, and therefore, our being (what we are and what we become). As such, it is not synonymous with religion even though it is intimately connected with it; the ultimate purpose of religion, in fact, is to unfold spirituality in its followers.

Religion, in general, provides us both with a partial representation, or image of spirituality, and with a set of teachings and principles by which man, after long and arduous efforts, will someday be able to achieve and realize spirituality.

A "picture," however, is not to be confused with the reality for which it stands. In the world, one may meet many athletes who are not training to become such, and one may find people in gymnasiums who are training themselves, but who are very far from being athletes. Similarly, religion should not be confused with spirituality which is its aim and ideal.

Moreover, religions are many while spirituality is essentially one; reality and truth are one, but there are many conceptual schemes to represent their various facets, aspects, and dimensions, just as there are many approaches and paths that lead to them.

Religions utilize different symbol systems, different conceptual schemes, and different approaches which are best suited to the people they serve, to lead them to the unfoldment and realization of their own spirituality. As such, religions are mainly culture bound.

Spirituality, on the other hand, being based upon a *direct personal experience* and realization of reality, is trans-cultural and truly universal, though expressing itself through many phases, degrees, and levels of realization.

What is generally viewed today as a "religious crisis," I see essentially as being a "spiritual crisis." At the root of this crisis stands the unfortunate fact that established religions are unable to show forth in their leaders and teachings examples of genuine and living spirituality. They fail to make their symbols and teachings meaningful, relevant, and practical for their followers, and therefore they are unable to foster and develop genuine spirituality in their members. Unfortunately, there are not enough Saints and Mystics to go around!

The answer to that crisis I see as being essentially "spiritual" rather than "religious", by that I mean we have to find or educate people who possess some degree of genuine spirituality, who will be drawn to an official religion, and who will be capable of interpreting into meaningful and practical terms the traditional symbols and teachings of religion and of offering a LIVING EXAMPLE of what a modern spiritual person can be.

Though spirituality is essentially a state of consciousness or awareness which must be achieved and personally experienced by an individual to be truly understood in its depths, certain of its general features and basic characteristics can be outlined intellectually; these are the following:

1. The general expression of spirituality.
2. The specific expression of spirituality.
3. The distinguishing features of spirituality.

The General Expression of Spirituality

At the general level, spirituality is the direct result and indicator of man's overall "maturity", or evolutionary status, on several levels. It is a cardinal assumption of the spiritual Tradition, which was taught openly by the Ancient Sages and by many religions, that man is composed of four "elements" and, therefore, he undergoes a fourfold development or evolution. These four "elements" were represented by the symbols of Earth, Water, Air and Fire which represent the physical, emotional, mental and spiritual dimensions of man's being and consciousness.

Man's fourfold evolution, or maturation process, can be traced and evaluated in terms of his 'four ages':

His Physical Age,
His Emotional Age,
His Mental Age,
His Spiritual Age.

Man's physical age is easily discerned by the number of chronological years that have elapsed since birth.

His emotional age can be determined by his capacity for

feeling, for empathy and sympathy, as well as by what he is emotionally drawn to and is attracting to himself.

One's mental age depends on one's capacity for thinking and reasoning, on his mental perception and alertness, on his ability to reason, to analyze, and to synthesize in a clear, cogent, and integrated fashion the various data and experiences which his attention has selected.

Finally, his spiritual age depends on the degree of spiritual consciousness which he has unfolded and on his capacity to grasp intuitively and to harmonize with the creative Source and Essence of his being, with the creative energies feeding and vitalizing his capacity to know, to love, and to create. In summary, to understand what he is, whence he came, whither he goes, and what is the purpose of this life on Earth and the specific concrete functions of his everyday experiences.

In its general expression, spirituality implies a certain amount of emotional, mental, and spiritual maturity, though not necessarily a certain physical age, such that spiritual consciousness—the awareness of one's Divine Spark and of Its will and Attributes—may freely and consciously express themselves through man's aspirations, thoughts, feelings, and will, and manifest in his life and behavior.

Spirituality implies that man's soul and its temporary dwelling place, the body, have become well developed and coordinated vehicles for the expression and manifestation, at the conscious level in this world, of man's spiritual nature and aspirations.

As such, the spiritual man becomes a natural 'leader' in whatever line of endeavor he gets involved with. From the outside, empirically, he can be observed to be highly vital, intelligent, and a very successful person. The functioning of his higher state of spiritual consciousness, operating through well coordinated mental and emotional vehicles and, possibly, though an equally well developed, strong and healthy body, gives him a distinct advantage in the struggle for survival and for self-affirmation in his everyday life.

Whatever situation in life a person who has developed a general level of spirituality may find himself in, whatever occupation, sport, or line of endeavor he may engage in, he is sure to succeed in it and to distinguish himself in a manner plainly visible to all.

The devotee does this by having a "passion for excellence", being committed to fulfill any task he finds himself involved in to the utmost of his human capacity, perceiving a deeper meaning and purpose behind all the seemingly trivial events of everyday life, and dedicating all his actions and under-takings not to "success" or to another human person, but to the birth and unfoldment of the God Within, and becoming vitalized and dynamized in His aspirations, thoughts, feelings and will by the spiritual energies.

The spiritual Man cannot avoid distinguishing himself and standing out as an unusual, highly vital, creative, re-sourceful, and capable person.

However, the empirical expressions or external manifes-tations of spirituality—inspiration, creative thinking, vital energies, resourcefulness, and success—do not represent and describe the heart and core of spirituality.

It is within the depths of the human psyche, in a purified and sanctified heart and mind alone, that the essence and true secrets of spirituality are revealed and experienced through a tremendous expansion of man's capacity to know and understand, to love and to feel, to create and to will, and not in his external behavior or achievements.

Thus to the unenlightened and inwardly unawakened person, spirituality is destined to remain an eternal mystery and enigma . . . until it will dawn and express itself within the core of his own inner being.

Strength, success, resourcefulness, and leadership are not by themselves indicators of spiritual realization and spiritual maturity as many concrete and historical examples have shown.

The Specific Expression of Spirituality

In contrast with the former, the specific expression of spirituality which is an earlier phase or stage of it, does not require a coordinated "maturity" or development of man's emotional, mental, and spiritual "ages" and "dimensions". What it does demand is the breakthrough and emergence of spiritual consciousness.

Thus a person may have achieved only a slight degree of emotional or mental development and still have experienced a genuine expression of spiritual consciousness, as witnessed by saints, seers, and religious leaders *who were far from being emotional or mental giants,* and who were certainly not 'balanced' in their emotional, mental, and spiritual manifestations.

That degree of balance, or proper coordination and harmonization of all of man's faculties around his spiritual consciousness is characteristic of the more advanced stage of general spirituality.

As it is quite apparent, man can be highly trained at the physical level (an athlete) without being equally developed at the emotional and mental levels; or he can be highly developed emotionally and sensitive (an artist) without being physically or mentally trained; finally, he can be highly mentally trained (an intellectual) without being physically or emotionally developed. The same is also true for the spiritual dimension and spiritual consciousness which can express themselves without necessarily requiring a high level of physical, emotional, and mental development and coordination. Man does not evolve at an even and harmonious pace and may show quite a descrepancy in his four ages.

In how one manifests the Divine Light, each person may show certain emphases and weak points. Spiritual Light is the source and essence of knowledge, love, and power; man, through different personal experiences and varying emphases on different psychospiritual Centers, may manifest different emphases upon knowledge, love, and power. Thus, in unfolding spirituality, one may temporarily travel along the *Path of Knowledge* (the Occultist), the *Path of Love* (the Mystic), or the *Path of Power* (the Magician).

At the higher levels of spiritual maturity, these paths must be properly fused and integrated, just as man's four ages must be balanced and integrated to become "awakened" and refined "instruments" of the Divine Spark which is consciously expressing Its Will and Attributes.

The Distinguishing Features of Spirituality

What are the major distinguishing features of spiritual consciousness which are qualitatively different from those of emotional and mental consciousness?

The following features constitute an inner, direct, and experiential realization of the individual in whom spiritual consciousness is blooming, and they carry with them a certainty, reality, and depth of experience that no external or intellectual teachings could ever impart. Briefly put, these are:

A. The deep experience and inner realization that one's True Self, the creative and living Source and Essence of one's being, which it is our destiny and task to consciously identify or unite with, is neither physical or psychic, but rather spiritual in its nature. As such, it is an immortal and integral part or "Spark" of the Cosmic Spirit which can never be destroyed or annihilated by any human experience and which must eventually reach its intended destiny: the conscious realization of Its perfection.

B. The deep experience and inner realization that life on Earth is good and infinitely valuable, that it is a great gift and a priceless opportunity for man to unfold all of his human powers and faculties and to become his true Self: a conscious, individualized creator; that this world was created by God, who is man's Father, as well as Love, Wisdom, and Creative Energy, and that this world is ruled down to its smallest and most "insignificant" details by Divine Providence; that ultimately, Divine Justice does prevail and that all human experiences have a purpose, a reason, and a meaning, which are "just and good".

There is no human experience, *bar none,* from which man cannot learn and benefit, *provided he approaches them in the proper frame of mind.*

C. The deep experience and inner realization that incarnation in this world and all human experiences therein, are ultimately, "means" or "lessons" by which man can find and unite with the God Within or the "unknown greater Self", and that all human activities and events should be dedicated to the Great Quest for God and the Great Work for a life more conscious, more full, and more abundant.

It is also the inner realization that the final yardstick to evaluate all human experiences and undertakings is not whether these are pleasant or unpleasant, successful or unsuccessful, rather whether they are helping or hindering, retarding or accelerating the birth and unfoldment of the Christ within, the dawning of genuine spiritual consciousness.

D. Finally, the realization and understanding of the daily tasks and lessons which the given person has come into incarnation to accomplish and a *consecration* of one's self, time, and resources to accomplish the mission, or set of tasks, one has come to carry out as fully as it is humanly possible.

What is the Spiritual or Primordial Tradition?

Unlike other human traditions such as the scientific, the philosophical, or even the theological which organize and articulate themselves in schools or societies and whose major assumptions, teachings, and philosophies are objectified and systematized in books and social institutions, the Spiritual Tradition is embodied and transmitted by *living human beings* who are generally not organized in formal institutions. It is expressed in the conscious experience and personal realization, in the soul, or psyche, of those who have attained a given level of spiritual consciousness or specific spirituality.

The spiritual or Primordial Tradition is completely universal and stretches all the way back to the dawn of human thinking and of human evolution; it is a living, dynamic, and unfolding vision and realization of human consciousness in which the spiritual level has become active in men and women of all races, religions and social strata. As such, it is a transcultural and non-institutionalized realization of the "Essence of Reality"—of God, man, and nature, and of their relationship and destiny—which certain human beings have achieved and which, ultimately, all human beings will achieve.

Its fundamental prerequisites are a certain spiritual age and "level of human consciousness and development" which, when achieved, admit a given human being into the great human spiritual brotherhood which exists on *both sides* of the grave, in this world where it must be earned and in the next, where it endures and is acknowledged.

Resting upon an inner revelation and realization which can only be personally experienced and which is a living, unfolding, and an ongoing process, its essence can never be expressed in books and dogmas, and its members (or adepts) cannot be organized into a "school" or "institution".

True, many fragments, symbols, and analogical representations of its basic tenets and realizations have been codified and objectified in various books, teachings, and thought systems, but its essence and living fundamentals which must by their very nature remain a *personal achievement* and a *personal experience,* have not been written down.

These partial fragments, images, and analogical representations have been organized and given to the world by three major sources:

1. The World Religions, which draw their very life and essence from them.
2. The Mystery Schools, which seek to train and qualify worthy and ready aspirants to its realizations and membership.
3. Individual Seers, Prophets, Poets, Saints, and Sages who have found literary, artistic, or philosophic media to convey their experiences and realizations of spiritual consciousness to other human beings, holding up before them a great ideal and a great promise which they, too, shall someday be able to realize.

The basic tenets and philosophy of the Spiritual Tradition, being rooted in a personal and direct experience and realization, can never be learned from sermons, books, or lectures, but only through the revelations and hierophanies of one's own Divine Spark.

Priests, Saints, Sages, and Initiates, who have themselves achieved a certain degree of spiritual awakening and of spiritual consciousness, enter the 'living stream' of the Primordial Tradition, but they cannot impart these treasures to their followers and loved ones; at best, they can only "prepare the way for He who is to come"—for the Christ Within, the Divine Spark, Who is the Great and only Hierophant of the Spiritual Mysteries.

Thus a young child in Tibet, an old woman in India, a businessman in America, a prisoner in Russia, and so on, may be linked with the Spiritual Tradition and become its carrier and living representative when genuine spiritual consciousness has begun to dawn in their psyche and illuminates their lives and beings. This can happen even if they have never heard the word before and if they never went to any school, church, or "Temple of the Mysteries", for they will have become "Initiates of its Mysteries" which is the only "badge of admission" which such a tradition has.

Were they to meet in the world, they would be able to recognize and to understand each other better than a mother or father understands his child, or the master his pupil, and the priest his faithful. This is because they have experienced the same reality and communed with the same Spirit which has revealed Its Mysteries to them, and not because they have attended the "same school". Moreover, they would instantly recognize each other by certain signs which their spiritual vision would reveal to them, which can never be faked, and which tell each their respective rank and status in the spiritual brotherhood of humanity.

The Spiritual or Primordial Tradition, therefore, is not an outer school or organization, but rather an inner achievement and realization; it is not based upon a particular teaching or book, but upon certain *specific experiences* and *developments of human consciousness;* it is not bound by race, time, or place, but it stretches out to embrace the whole of humanity in a living, growing, unfolding synthesis of spiritual consciousness; it can never to taught or conferred *outside* in the world, but only obtained by one's efforts, achievements, and maturity *within oneself.*

Rather than being a group of people discussing certain tenets, teachings, or books of the "Masters", it is a brotherhood of personal experience and existential realization or "Initiation". Its members have not gone to the "same school" or joined the "same society", and thus they are not unified by its "classics" or by its "constitution," rather, they are more like a club of alpinists or explorers who have climbed the same mountains and explored the same country even if by different paths and in different degrees.

It is not words, ideas, or principles shared in common that unites them and enables them to communicate with and understand each other, but a shared set of experiences, the partaking of the same reality and communing with the same spirit. This fact raises an interesting problem and points to a cardinal teaching of the Spiritual Tradition, namely, that truth, unity, brotherhood, and a genuine cognitive synthesis of reality and of all human experience (which is the most profound, vital, and ambitious of all undertakings of human knowledge), together with the solution of the most fundamental problems of humanity:

The Riddle of the Sphinx,

The Mystery of Life,

The Enigma of the Universe,

cannot be realized and attained by the "natural man", but only by the "spiritual man"; that the most vital and important questions of human knowledge and curiosity cannot be contained or satisfied by science, philosophy, or theology which operate mainly through the intellectual dimension, but only by a personal spiritual awakening and an initiation into spiritual consciousness by the "Spiritual Tradition" living in the heart and soul of the purified and regenerated human being.

This is another reason why it has been said: "Seek ye first the Kingdom of Heaven (i.e. spiritual consciousness) and all these things shall be added unto you" and "the wisdom of the world (i.e. natural consciousness) is foolishness (i.e. incomplete and lacking in essence) in the eyes of God (i.e. of the spiritually illuminated and awakened consciousness), Who can reveal His Mysteries in the heart of a child" (i.e. in the consciousness of one who though young in biological years is old in spiritual maturity).

How I Became Involved With These "Adventures" and How You Too, Can do the Same

As a child, and even more so as an adolescent, I was a very restless, dissatisfied, and lonely person with powerful energies and drives flowing through my being which neither my parents nor I could really understand and cope with adequately.

The answers to the endless questions about myself and why I was the way I was, about life, and about the 'why of things' which I got from my parents, teachers, and clergy did not satisfy me and did not 'fit in' with my own personal experiences and with the realizations of my inner consciousness.

Something undefined, yet most important was missing, something which could best be described as a "yearning for substance and reality, for completeness and synthesis" was lacking. This undefined hunger, this profound dissatisfaction with the world views and basic answers I was given, this "inner substantial poverty" was the motivating spring which launched me on a 'metaphysical quest' for Truth, for Being, and for a life more full, abundant, and consciously lived.

After voracious reading and endless discussions with a wide variety of people, and long travels in many countries spiced with many experiences, I soon came to the conclusion that science, philosophy, and religion, did not have the answers I was seeking, and could not satisfy my deep inner hunger for knowing and understanding.

At this point, I vowed to myself that I would spend most of my life and resources to find these answers wherever they could be found and under whatever labels or symbols they might be couched, and to articulate them and develop them for myself, if I could find them in the world.

After a long and rather dry period, punctuated by more traveling and experiences, I came across certain books on Eastern Yoga and 'world mysticism', which set my heart on fire and my mind in a state of great ferment. Here at last, in

black and white, I found a correspondence and conceptualiz-
ation of the deepest truths and insights I had earlier found in
my own psyche.

This proved to me that I was not alone in this quest and
that other, well known and respected human beings, had
experienced even to a greater extent what I had experienced
or intuited vaguely but compellingly. Thus, I set upon a new
program of study and went about collecting as many books as
I could find in Paris, London, and New York. After a while, I
became satiated with books and longed to meet the human
beings who had written them, these people who had lived and
personally experienced these things, and who could therefore,
guide me and advise me on my quest.

After an extended and fruitless search, characteried by
many disappointments and "crashing pedestals", when I
least expected it, but most needed it, I met the first genuine
mystic . . . and through her three or four others . . .

Recognizing a profound kinship with such people and
also that they knew and realized far more than I, I set out
seeking to unfold within myself what I recognized and
admired in them. Their most unanimous and persistant
warning, however, was that they could not teach me or give
me what I hungered for, but merely *point the way* to what I
should do to unfold spiritual consciousness in myself.

After many years of reading and experimentation, and
many, many experiences of all kinds, I finally began to
realize that the answers to the riddles and mysteries I sought
could only come from *within* myself through a personally
lived experience and realization and not from the outside,
from books, words, or lectures.

Then, as some of these mysteries and riddles began to
unveil their deeper meanings and implications, I marveled at
the greatness, wisdom and love of God, at the beauty and
preciousness of life, at the great opportunities which knock
at the door of our consciousness everyday. I marveled at the

Divine Justice which underpins all human events and experiences and I embarked upon one of the most fascinating, stimulating, and life giving of all human experiences—*the spiritual adventure.* I also realized experientially the truth of the old saying of Angelus Silesius: "If that which thou seekest thou findest not within thyself, thou wilt surely not find it without."

Chapter Four

THE SEVEN FUNDAMENTALS
AND THE
PRIMORDIAL TRADITION

One of the central problems which all religions must face is
that of their validity and universality. We ask:

> To whom are the teachings and symbols of a given
> religion applicable?
> What is the relationship of this religion to the other
> religions?
> How are its basic dogmas, creed, and rituals to be
> viewed—as a set of universal truths and divine
> revelations valid for all human beings in all historical
> periods, or as a set of sociocultural products valid
> only for certain people at a certain point of their
> historical development?
> Is there a common core and a common source for
> man's various religious approaches and churches?

These are some of the basic questions and problems inherent
to and raised by all great religions which we shall examine in
this chapter.

Interestingly enough, all great religions have more or
less stated in their pantheon and theology a monothestic
conception of God, the conception of One God, the "Father

of the Gods" or an "Unknown God". It is from this conception that arose the universal notion of the "Fatherhood of God" and of the "Brotherhood of Men", i.e. that all men come from the same source eventually to return to it, which would indeed make them "spiritual and human brothers".

This monotheistic conception implies that the Supreme Reality, both inside and outside of man, is One, and that human beings may have access to that One Reality wherein the true and final basis for human understanding, human sympathy, and human cooperation is to be found. As one spiritual school tersely put it: "We affirm that the mortal may attain to the knowledge of the spiritual while yet incarnate."*

If God, the Supreme Reality, the Source and Essence of all there is and the destiny of Man, is One, then the symbolic descriptions, the intellectual representations of the Paths, techniques, and ethics which lead thereto are many.

As an old Vedic Text puts it: "God is One but men call Him by many names."

The forms and the interpretations of divine revelation and of the breakthrough of the superconscious into the conscious are, likewise, many. As the great German Mystic Karl von Eckartshausen writes:

> But, when men multiplied, the frailty of man and his weakness necessitated an exterior society which veiled the interior one, and concealed the spirit and the truth in the letter. The people at large were not capable of comprehending high interior truth, and the danger would have been too great in confiding that which was of all most holy to incapable people. Therefore, inward truths were wrapped in external and viable ceramonies, so that men, by the perception of the outer, which is the symbol of the interior, might by degree be enabled to safely approach the interior spiritual truths. †

Thus not only are there many religions and many theologies with different symbol systems, metaphysical systems, and ethical systems, but even within the same

---

*SRIA Documents
† Cloud Upon the Sanctuary, p. 18

religion are many denominations, splinters, and different interpretations of the same source of revelation.

On the one hand, this is because God (the Spirit) does not "speak" directly and conceptually to men and, on the other hand, because men, even great and inspired men, Prophets and Mystics, receive Divine Revelation in accordance with their receptivity for it and translate it and interpret it in terms of their own level of consciousness, background of experience, and general understanding of man and life. Thus revelations and theophanies are always differently received and interpreted and therefore, "colored", by the human consciousness through which they manifest.

This process goes through two basic phases:

1. We have the coloring and the interpretation of this revelation by the receptivity and level of human consciousness, of its 'vehicle' (the Prophet or Mystic).

2. We have the different understanding, interpretation, and systematization of the revelation and experiences of the Prophet or Mystic by his followers and apologists.

Behind the various theoretical interpretations and rationalizations of a given religion's "revelation" and, in fact, behind the revelation of all religions, stands a fundamental core of truths, principles, and insights which are universal and valid for all men of all times and places. As Karl von Echartshausen writes:

> Meanwhile, a more advanced school has always existed to which the deposition of all science has been confided, and this school was the community illuminated interiorly by the Savior, the society of the Elect, which has continued from the first day of creation to the present times; its members, it is true, are scattered all over the world, but they have always been united by one spirit and one truth; they have had but one knowledge, a single source of truth; one Lord, one doctor, and one master, in whom resides substantially the whole plentitude of God, who also alone initiates them into the high mysteries of Nature and of the Spiritual World . . .

> This community of light has existed since the first day of the world's

creation, and its duration will be to the end of time. It is the society of those elect who know the Light in the Darkness and separate what is pure therein. This community possesses a school in which all who thirst for knowledge are instructed by the Spirit of Wisdom itself; and all the mysteries of God and of Nature are preserved therein for the children of light. Perfect knowledge of God, of nature, and of humanity are the objects of instruction in this school. It is thence that all truths penetrate into the world; herein is the School of the Prophets and of all who search for wisdom; it is in this community alone that truth and the explanation of all mystery is to be found. It is the most hidden of communities, yet it possesses members gathered from many orders . . .

From all time, therefore, there has been a hidden assembly, a society of the elect, of those who sought for and had a capacity for Light, and this interior society was called the interior Sanctuary or Church. All that the external Church possesses in symbol, ceremony or rite is the letter which expresses externally the spirit and the truth residing in the interior Sanctuary . . .

The wisdom of the temple under the ancient alliance was preserved by the priests and by the prophets. To the priests was confided the external, the cortex of hieroglyph. The prophets had the charge of the inner truth, and their occupation was continually to recall the priests from the letter to the spirit when they began to forget the spirit and cleave only to the letter. The science of the priests was that of the knowledge of exterior symbols. That of the prophets was experimental possession of the truth of the symbols. In the external was the letter; in the interior the spirit lived. There was, therefore, in the ancient alliance a school of prophets and of priests, the one occupying itself with the spirit in the emblem, the other with the emblem itself . . .

The external Church of the ancient alliance was visible; the interior Church was always invisible, must be invisible, and yet must govern all, because force and power are alone confided to her.*

The spirit and the heart behind the symbols and the teachings of all religions has been known by many names and many labels. The best known of these are:

> the "Philosophia Perennis"
> the "Hagia Sophia"
> the "Primordial Tradition"

Cloud Upon the Sanctuary, pp. 15, 16, 22.

the "Spiritual and Mystical Tradition."

This core of universal principles and truths is not static and fixed but dynamic and unfolding; it continually grows and expands on its foundation, not denying it but rendering it fuller and more complete.

To get at this universal core behind all religions is to be able to discern and to separate the elements and dimensions which are man-made and, therefore, culture-bound, relating to time and place, and level of evolution, from those which are truly universal, spiritual, and absolute.

As the sacred texts of every religion tell us, this is not a matter of studying texts and commentaries, it is a question of expanding one's level of consciousness; for it is not the ability to reason and scholarship that can reveal these hidden truths but only the Spirit of God working through the superconscious.

All the fundamental documents, prayers, and rituals of the world religions do contain both elements which are intermingled together and which coexist simultaneously at different levels—the spiritual and the human, the absolute and the relative.

Analytically speaking, there are three major approaches one can take to religion:

the *emotional* or existential

the *intellectual* or theoretical

the *spiritual* or esoteric.

The emotional or existential approach, consists basically in joining a given religion, in participating in its community life and in seeking to implement its ethical system and its practical teachings as much as it is humanly possible.

The intellectual or theoretical approach, consists not in becoming a member of any one particular religion, but in studying and analyzing its "sacred book", commentaries, and practical teachings in the light of natural reason and in comparison with other religions.

The third approach, the spiritual or esoteric, is that of the Initiate, who is capable of deciphering its key symbols, of lifting (at least partially) the veil of its mysteries, and of experiencing some of its great treasures and promises.

It is also interesting to note how the first and second approaches deal essentially with the world of multiplicity, with the dimension of the many clashing and opposing religions and denominations, while the third deals essentially with the world of unity, with the dimension of the one living stream of spirituality.

Thus it is priests, theologians, and fanatic "true believers" who fight about religion and who seek to promulgate their own religion as the "One True Religion" as against all the other "false" religions.

True Mystics and Initiates of the spiritual Tradition look beyond the image of the symbols and the analogical garments of a particular form of revelation to its inner core and living foundation in reality which is indeed one.

Most great Western Religions have always claimed that they are universally valid and that they are the One True Religion, and according to the level at which this claim is interpreted, it is both true and false. There is a common universal core to these religions which is universally valid, and there is "One, Holy, Catholic Church", which is the source-root whence all religions have drawn their mystical core.

This core, as Eckartshausen tells us, has existed since the first day of the world's creation, and its duration will be to the end of time, until all human beings have been spiritually regenerated and have found a conscious and full union with God.

This *Inner Church* has inspired and guided all world religions, providing them with their central mystical core and with their great symbolic blueprints, but it has never been and and will never be fully incarnated and institutionalized on

Earth.

Let us now turn to true spiritual work, to this mystical core, as it is represented, (in a symbolic and veiled fashion) by all religions and in a more direct and rational fashion by the Mystery Schools. The central aim of the spiritual development and of spiritual growth, and of life on Earth, is to lead man to consciously achieve a fuller being and to live a fuller life. The ultimate aim is to lead man by degrees to become *actually,* in the here and now of his Earthly life, what he is *potentially:* A Spiritual Being, a Son of God.

At the practical level, spiritual training and growth have two central objectives, both for one's self and for the others. These are: *Illumination* and *Healing.* Both involve becoming evermore aware of the Light, and suffusing oneself (one's Aura and Tree of Life) with the spiritual Light which will then transform us into new beings. Both are intimately related to each other as illumination implies raising one's level of consciousness and one's life to higher, more real and vital levels, and as healing implies making the sick well again so that they might then grow towards greater heights of consciousness and levels of being.

Worship (Prayer in its ritualistic or theurgic part) is anchored upon seven major documents or blueprints in the Western Spiritual Tradition which have their equivalents or correspondences in the Eastern Tradition or in any genuine spiritual Tradition for that matter.

In these documents one can find, if one searches deeply enough, all the basic knowledge of God, man, and nature, and their relationships to one another.

One can also find in them all the symbols needed for concentration, meditation, and contemplation, and all the practical exercises which are necessary to achieve genuine spiritual consciousness and the Birth of the Christ within. These constitute the very heart and subtance of the Western Spiritual Tradition and contain enough information and practical exercises to lead any human being from the state of nature to the state of grace (from a human to a spiritual state).

These seven great documents or fundamentals are:

1. Divine Names
2. The Sign of the Cross
3. The Lord's Prayer
4. The Nicene Creed
5. The Beatitudes
6. The Hail Mary
7. The Ten Commandments

Each of these documents and glyphs is an autonomous unit and is complemented, reinforced, and completed by the others; each contains in the inner structure its symbols and relationships:

A simple and practical system of spiritual development and self-realization.

A cognitive system containing a philosophy of man, of his being, origin, and destiny.

An integrated set of psychospiritual exercises designed to awaken and activate certain Centers on the Tree of Life, to open up certain "doors" and "layers" of consciousness, and to *stimulate certain energies* into activity—to alter and expand human consciousness and to lead to the dawning of genuine spiritual consciousness through a progressive purification, consecration, and illumination of man's Tree of Life and Aura.

A blueprint for formulating and realizing ideals, the art of thought-form creation, projection, and realization.

Chapter Five

DIVINE NAMES:
THEIR NATURE AND USE

From time immemorial there has been known to all advanced students of the Mysteries, to Prophets, Mystics, and Initiates of all races and ages, an arcane Art and Science based on the use of *Names of Power.*

This Art and Science of self-actualization and spiritual Initiation has been called by many names and has assumed many forms and expressions. In the East is is best known under the name of *Mantra Yoga* while in the West it is called *Theurgy* by the Occult Schools and *The Way of the Name* by the Mystic Schools.

This method of using Names of Power is most important for anyone who is seriously interested in spiritual work and who is ready for it; this is because it constitutes the first and most important pillar of all true spiritual science, whether of the East or of the West, in the Lesser or in the Greater Mysteries, on the Occult as well as on the Mystical Path. This method will be used by the aspirant to the Mysteries from his first entry on the Path, where he shall find it at its very "door", all the way through his final achievement of Christhood or Spiritual Illumination. As such, it is also the first and the most important of the seven keys to full spiritual growth and Initiation.

The use of Names of Power is an art as well as a science, for it contains theoretical principles which are true for all men and practical applications which yield results that are both universal at one level, and unique to the practitioner at another. As a science, this method can be described and formalized in a theoretical scheme, but as an art it can only be personally lived and experienced.

Why are names so important, not only in the psychic and spiritual fields, but also in everyday life? Because the capacity to name things implies, among other things, the power of reason, a language, *human consciousness*, which are man's distinctive traits as a human being. This capacity has been with us from the very beginning of man's evolution on Earth and will remain with us until the end of our evolution here.

In Genesis we find God telling man to give a name to all the creatures of the air, sea, and earth, and to all the objects of creation. We find again and again in all the sacred scriptures, a very strong value being put upon God revealing His Name to His servants.

The religious importance of God's Name was so great that there is even one of the Ten Commandments which urges men not to "take the Name of the Lord God in vain."

The Lord's Prayer, which is another important key to spiritual training in the West, also contains one special petition or formula: "Hallowed be Thy Name".

Finally, one of the external clues by which one can discern a true student of the Mysteries is that he will never use lightly or irreverently *any* Divine Name for he knows, by his own personal experience, their power and holiness.

In our present civilization we can readily see how important it is to name a child when he is born and know the name (and the address) of a person we would like to get in touch with.

The name and labeling of people and of things is of such importance that science is constantly coining new names for what it discovers. Furthermore, to know someone or something, we must know his name. Without names there would be no language and no systematic knowledge of anything; and without language there would be no reason and no human consciousness, and without these there would be no human beings. Conversely, looking towards the future, we could say that without knowing and using Divine Names man would find it difficult to know God and continue his human evolution towards spiritual evolution and to achieve his eventual union with God.

It is simple to see why names are so important for man. They are symbols, psychic media, which convey and elicit the various units of human consciousness which we call intuitions, thoughts, feelings, and vital energies. They are the true "units" of human consciousness, "streams of focused ideas and emotions", and "bundles of energy". They are the lens which direct and focus our whole attention upon one aspect of reality, upon one power or being.

These Divine Names function as catalysts which awaken certain energies and states of consciousness in our psyche.

In short, they are psychospiritual means by which we invoke a certain Presence, induce a certain state of consciousness, and focus our awareness; by which we recreate in ourselves an image, or facsimile, of that which is outside or above us.

Names are so important to man in all his activities, both sacred and profane, because they are the means by which man deliberately awakens and focuses his intuitions, thoughts, and energies by an effort of the will.

Names, therefore, are the key regulators and switches of man's human consciousness and of his inner life. It is through Names (words, images, symbols, sounds) that all alterations, directing, focusing, and expansion of human consciousness take place. For Names guide and direct the mind, and it is a well known esoteric fact that the mind takes on the form of the object it beholds and that the vital energies of man's being run along the lines traced by the mind, energizing the things, or areas, about which we think.

A Word of Power is an ideal, containing various psychological energies and materials (intuitions, thoughts, feelings, and vital energies) which are crystallized and concretized, projected by the will and the imagination, and then introjected into the psyche so that temporarily, the operator can identify with it and serve as a channel to manifest its attributes and energies in the world.

It is names, whether in religion, poetry, literature, esoteric science, or even everyday speech, that bring about the magic of inducing certain thoughts, feelings, and moods.

By the proper use of Names man can feel surprised, frightened, soothed, excited, joyful, or depressed. He can learn and teach, enlighten or confuse, direct others or be directed.

The power of names upon the human psyche and human behavior is positively staggering. This fact has now been recognized by theology, sociology, psychology, spiritual science, and even common sense.

The Holy Scriptures, mythologies, legends, and great masterpieces of world literature are all replete with countless references and hints about "miraculous" and "magical" power of Holy Names, be they that of Krishna, Buddha, Mithras, Osiris, Yahve, or Jesus. Both religious and mystical traditions have numerous and very explicit statements concerning the importance of Divine Names. Thus, to cite just a few examples:

    1. A Buddhist Psalm tells its devotees: "There is no way into the Kingdom of Gladness save only by attaining unto the true faith through that Holy Name, the very Jewel of Wonder . . . the Holy Name of

Buddha, of that Boundless Light that shineth into all the worlds of the Ten Regions, and the glory of His Kingdom destroys the darkness of ignorance in the Eternal Night, thus fulfilling all the longings of men."*

2. In the Christian Bible, Old and New Testament alike, we find a profusion of similar references, descriptions, and hints. Thus we have, for instance: "They that love Thy Name shall be joyful in Thee" (Psalm 5:12). "Thy Name is an ointment poured forth . . . draw me, we will run after Thee" (Zech. 10:22). "I will glorify Thy Name for evermore" (Psalm 86:12). "They have built Thee a sanctuary therein for Thy Name" (II Chron. 20:8).

3. Jesus explicitly emphasized the power of Holy Names when He told His Disciples: "Whatsoever ye shall ask the Father in my Name, He will give it to you. Hitherto ye have asked nothing in My Name: ask and ye shall receive" (John 16:23-24). "When two or three are gathered together in My Name there I am in the midst of them" (Matt. 18:20). And "In My Name shall they cast out devils; they shall speak with new tongues . . . They shall lay hands on the sick, and they shall recover" (Mark 16:17-18).

4. The Mystical Tradition of the Eastern Church, known as the Hesychast Tradition, is well known to have anchored its search for spiritual enlightenment around the "Way of the Name", or the Jesus Prayer, as it is better known. This tradition has accorded explicit importance to the practice of the Holy Name which is used as the primary means to expand consciousness. Here the Holy Name is that of Jesus Christ, embedded in the short exclamation:

"O Lord Jesus Christ, Son of God, Savior, have

---

*SRIA Documents

mercy upon me."
This formula has many versions, the shortest of which is the single word "Jesus".
This mantram, accompanied by the Sign of the Cross, is repeated over and over again by the devotee with different techniques of breathing, visualization, and concentration until his state of consciousness noticeably alters.

5.   An Eastern contemplative who used this method writes: "The Name Itself is a means of purification and perfection, a touchstone, a filter through which our thoughts, words, and deeds have to pass to be freed of other impurities. None of them ought to be admitted by us until we pass them through the Name, and the Name excludes all sinful elements. Only that will be received which is compatible with the Name of Jesus. We shall fill our hearts to the brim with the Name and thought of Jesus, holding it carefully like a precious vessel and defending it against all alien tampering and admixture. This is severe asceticism. It requires a forgetfulness of self, a dying to self, as the Holy Name grows in our souls and gives us a foretaste of what spiritual power really is."*

6.   And the same contemplative concludes:
When we separately consider the aspects or implications of the Name of Jesus, our invocation of the Name is like a prism which splits up a beam of white light into several colors of the spectrum. When we call on the "total Name" we are using the Name as a lens which receives and concentrates the white light. Through the means of a lens a ray of the sun can ignite some combustible substance. The Holy Name, acting as a lens, can gather and direct the light until a fire is kindled within us." †

Likewise, the Mystery Schools and the Occult and

---

*Invocation, Its Fundamentals and Practice (Sundial House, 1973) p. 10.
† Ibid., p. 32.

Magical Traditions have the same basic teaching concerning the use of Words of Power, but they couch it in different words and use different techniques. Thus the Tree of Life, which is the master glyph and the practical "workshop" of the Western Spiritual Tradition (as well as being the blueprint of man's psychic and spiritual anatomy and the diagrammatic exposition of the universe) is activated in each of its 10 Sephiroth—on the Four Worlds by the Name of Power.

To activate each of the 10 Centers and to travel the 32 Paths that connect them, the Initiate vibrates the Names of the Gods, Archangels, and Angels attributed to them. It is upon these Names of Spiritual Power that the Initiate draws upon to cooperate with the Divine Purpose and to consciously speed up his human and spiritual evolution—to create, complete, and perfect both himself and the world.

By vibrating a given Name of Power in a Center, in one of the Worlds, the Initiate actually suffuses his spiritual and psychic anatomy with the Light and Energies corresponding to that Power, attracting into his Aura the highest essence and energies of that Plane and Power. This is the reason why the Neophyte of the Mystery Schools is solemnly admonished: "By Names and Images are all Powers awakened and reawakened" and that "Names of Power link one spiritually to the Beings who are invoked and who become aware of that invocation".

In the Christian Church we find a parallel to the foregoing both in the office of *Prothesis of the Orthodox Liturgy* and in the *Rosary of the Roman Catholic Church.* In the first, every Spiritual Hierarchy, from the Holy Trinity to Angels are invoked by Name, while in the second, various Names of Gods, Angels, and Saints are also invoked and verbally ejaculated several times for the same purpose, but without explaining why they are doing so.

The Hesychast Tradition, previously mentioned, also

claims that the Name of Jesus vibrated in the human heart, from which it radiates and propagates like a true spiritual sun in every cell and department of our little kingdom, gives it the "power of deification".

Thus, it is no wonder that the sacred axiom of the Brotherhood of the Rosy Cross enscribed on the vault of the Adepts is "Jesus is my All" which, when uttered with FAITH (Concentration, Understanding, and Love) brings the living Presence of Jesus not only in our hearts, but from there, to every Center and cell of our being.

Like the legendary archetype of the Order, Christian Rosy Cross, the advanced student of the Mysteries must learn to say, to experience and to realize: "Jesus is my all and His Name is the Mystery of my Salvation".

Apostolic Christianity, likewise, vouches explicitly and through many of its Saints for the Power of the Holy Name of Jesus to "cast out devils", to "heal the sick", to "speak in new tongues", and to attain to the Living Presence, i.e. to genuine spiritual Initiation.

Why do words of Power act in such a way and why is the Name of Jesus so important for the student of the Western Spiritual Tradition? Words of power act as psychic lenses to focus all of man's psychic energies upon one central object.

In making a powerful effort of the will and in giving of himself, man will also receive from his own Divine Spark and from the forces of the cosmos drawn into him by the principle of "like attracts like".

By offering the best of himself, his human consciousness, knowledge, love, and vital energies focused and directed through a Name, man will receive from his own Divine Spark and from the Higher Planes, a vaster knowledge, a deepened love, and vitalized energies. In short, he will become, through a transformation and expansion of consicousness and a changed way of life, A NEW BEING.

The key to using Names of Power effectively is to become united with *and a channel for* the Power which the Name represents, to make the "Word become flesh"; in other words, to enable the consciousness and life for which the Name represents to find a channel through one's human consciousness so as to manifest their attributes and carry out their will on the physical plane.

The specific process by which this is accomplished is the following: The Name or Word is merely a vehicle, a cup or chalice, for the life and consciousness which must fill it. It is this consciousness, or Spirit, which gives the Name life, meaning, and power; it is this Spirit which expands and unfolds from Plane to Plane to the Divine Plane itself.

The construction of the "chalice" of the Name on the Inner Planes, and the formation of its thoughtform in the Astral Light involves the use of man's power of concentration and visualization, of meditation and adoration, of invocation and evocation. But the ensoulment of that "chalice" or "mould" in the Astral Light is the result of an answer to man's desire and longing for it; it is the fulfillment of man's love call for the Light by the free gift of the Spirit which pours Its life into it.

Thus it is, that the form of the Name, its chalice, image and color, is the product of the human will, concentration, adoration, and visualization; while its ensoulment or "coming to life" is the result of man's faith and love and of God's free gift and expression of Himself; it is the product of the complete operation of uniting one's psyche with the Power behind the Name and of making the Word become flesh (offering one's psyche and body as Its temple). This process involves both maximum human effort and a free manifestation of the Light which can in no way be coerced or brought down into manifestation.

Using Names of Power was explicitly hinted at in the

story of the three Magi coming to worship the Christ child and in the greatest of all Commandments.

The Magi, representing the royal and distinctive characteristics of human nature—knowledge, love, and will—must worship the Christ child (the manifestation of the Divine Spark) by offering Gold, Myrrh, and Frankincense (the best of human knowledge, human love, and human energies) which are then transformed, exalted, and spiritualized.

The Commandment of Commandments: "Thou shalt love the Lord thy God with all thy heart (love), all thy soul (will), and all thy mind (knowledge)," points to exactly the same process; a process which was also symbolically decribed by the Mystery Schools in the Alchemical operation utilizing Mercury (knowledge), Sulphur (love), and Salt (will), to produce the Azoth or the *Elixir Vitae,* the higher spiritual consciousness.

The entity, or thoughtform, which man has thus constructed will then become, according to his FAITH (concentration, understanding and love), the Door or Channel through which the Divine Light of God, and all the corresponding vibrations in the Cosmos, will pour forth upon the devotee and suffuse him (when the Name used is that of JESUS CHRIST) with the Divine Wisdom of the Father, the Divine Love of the Son, and the Divine Creative Energies of the Holy Spirit in a *Cross pattern* which will slowly spread to all the Centers, cells, and departments of his being, until every nook and corner of his little Kingdom have been filled with the Light, Life and Love of God. Then the subjective element (man's human consciousness) becomes united with the objective element (the Spiritual Light), the Word with the Spirit, the conscious with the superconscious, and man with God, as aspiration is answered by inspiration and invocation by evocation.

A Word of Power (and the Holy Name of Jesus Christ in particular) is a "seed" or "stone", a "light-bulb" in us that has to become alive in us once it has been 'planted', until it expands so as to encompass all of our being, making our human consciousness the Temple for Its Spirit and a *Living Rosy Cross.*

In order that this supreme operation may be effective and properly realized, the candidate must first purify, develop, and integrate his etheric, astral, and mental bodies; for man's highest mental vibrations become the point of ingress for Divine Wisdom, as his highest emotions become the point of ingress for Divine Creative Energies.

Each Name can be seen as possessing three basic dimensions: the physical, the psychic, and the spiritual which are given life and power by the Father, Son, and the Holy Spirit. On the physical level, the Name is most often handed down to us through the sacred texts or by the sacred traditions. On the spiritual level, the Name is given Life and Power by the Spirit which begets it. But on the psychic level, it must be forged and fashioned in our human consciousness to act as a channel between the Spirit and Matter, the superconscious and the conscious, by the conscious use of all our psychological faculties.

A point to be made here is that a Name must not only be concretized in the Astral Light by concentration and visualization but also fed and amplified by meditation and adoration if it is to become ensouled and given life by the Spirit, in contemplation.

This means that the student must meditate *regularly* on the Name he is building; that he must seek to "link" the Name to what he knows, to what he is, to what he is doing in his daily life, and to what he is striving to become. He must uncover and make explicit the many meanings, implications, and correspondences the Name has for him personally.

He must set it at the center of his attention and then "free associate" with the Name of Power by letting all intuitions, thoughts, and feelings associated with the Name flow through his stream of awareness. For only then will the Name become a true Name of Power for him, by expanding its meaning and revealing its deeper mysteries as the student's consciousness expands and unfolds.

Seen in this light, the Science and Art of Divine Names also becomes a primary way of developing the student's power of concentration, meditation, and contemplation.

At the physical level the student must learn how to concentrate his whole being (all his heart, soul, and mind) on the chosen Name, making it the primary focus of his attention to the exclusion of all else.

At the psychic level, he should meditate upon it, free associating around it, and turning it into a "filing cabinet" for all incoming intuitions, thoughts, and feelings relating to it.

All meanings, associations, and implications which are revealed to the student should then be integrated with what he knows, what he is, and what he hopes to become.

At the spiritual level, he should contemplate the Name, pouring his love and life into it and receiving greater love and life from its Spirit, and becoming a channel for its conscious expression in the world.

The Name used in this fashion then becomes a true "door" for its Spirit, its Life, and its Consciousness, which becomes an objective Presence and Reality to the student and which can act as a lens or filter for all his thoughts, emotions, intuitions, sensations, moods, and decisions.

As the student grows and matures, becoming more and more proficient in the use of Names of Power, he will eventually discover that, at their source, all Divine Names can be found in One Name, and that the Spirit behind them is, indeed, One and Universal.

As the late renowned Occultist Dion Fortune stated so many times: "In One God there is all the Gods and behind all the Gods and Goddesses there is One God."

Karl von Eckartshausen put it even better:

As infinity in number loses itself in the unit which is their basis, and as the innumerable rays of a circle are united in a single center, so it is with the Mysteries; their hieroglyphs and infinitude of emblems have the object of exemplifying but one single truth. He who knows this has found the key to understand everything and all at once. There is but one God, but one Truth, and one way which leads to this grand Truth. There is but one means of finding it. He who has discovered this way possesses everything therein; all wisdom in one book alone, all strength in one force, every beauty in one single object, all riches in one treasure only, every happiness in one perfect felicity. And the sum of all these perfections is Jesus Christ.*

This brings us to our next question: The use of the Divine Name of Jesus Christ and why it is so special.

To the student of the Mysteries there are many Divine Names and many Names of Power that are highly relevent and effective (The Names of the Trinity: Father, Son, and Holy Spirit; the Name of the Theotokus, Mary; the Name of the Celestial Hierarchs and of the Saints, and the whole range of the Qabalistic Names of Power).

But amongst all these, there is One very special and potent Name of Power, that of Jesus Christ. As the New Testament puts it: "God hath highly exalted Him and given Him a Name which is above every Name . . . that at the Name of Jesus every knee shall bow" (Phil. 2:9-10). And: "Neither there is Salvation in any other, for there is none other Name under heaven given among men whereby we must be saved." (Acts 4:12).

The translation of the word Jesus means *Savior* and that of the name of *Christ* means "the Anointed One," the "Messiah." That is exactly what the Supreme Name of Power should mean to every student of the Mysteries: salvation through the coming and at-onement with the Anointed One, the Christ within.

If to the first axiom of the Brotherhood of the Rosy Cross: "He is my all and His Holy Name is the Mystery of

---

Cloud Upon the Sanctuary

my Salvation" we then add its second axiom: "Jesus Christ, Man and God," we shall have a direct hint as to the esoteric meaning and impact of the Holy Name. Jesus Christ is the archetype and the prototype for every human being—what we, too, at the end of our earthly evolution, must and will become.

He, "Jesus Christ", is our supreme Ideal and Savior. Jesus can be seen as the symbol of the human side of our nature, as the *Temple* or set of coordinated vehicles (physical, emotional, mental, and spiritual). We must build for the Divine Spark in us, so that It can become conscious of Itself and manifest Its attributes of Divine Love, Divine Wisdom, and Divine Creative Energies in Creation.

Christ can be seen as the symbol of the Divine side of our nature, as our very own Divine Spark, or "Only Begotten Son of God," as the Bible has it.

"Jesus" is our "Savior" for many reasons, chiefly:

1. Because He represents the perfected, fully actualized and completed man; what we have to strive for and will eventually become.

2. Because the only true Salvation for man lies in going boldly forward towards a greater actualization of our human faculties and realization of our spiritual potentialities.

   The most important questions for all human beings (Who am I? Where do I come from? Why am I here? Why are certain things happening to me? How should I live? What should I aim for?) can only be answered through the realization of spiritual consciousness. Man can neither go back in the past nor stand still in the present; He must go boldly forward to find a new, greater, and more conscious harmony than the one he lost (in the Garden of Eden when he was living "in nature"). And if he is to go forward, he must know what he is to become; he must have a Supreme Ideal for his Self of tomorrow, and that supreme Ideal is embodied in the person, life and teaching of Jesus. Finally, the salvation, not only of the individual, but also of the Angelic beings also resides with man's achievement of full manhood, and man's realizing his perfection, which is to become 'Jesus'.

"Christ", on the other hand, is our Divine Spark, which is the "Anointed One" in our complex nature, an integral "Spark" or "Nucleus" of the Universal spirit. He is the "Only Begotten Son of God", and the reason why our complex nature, lower and higher, has evolved and is evolving in its earthly pilgrimage.

"Christ" (our Divine Spark) is the only One Who can truly "initiate us", grant us true peace and happiness, and open the Gates of Heaven (the higher states of spiritual consciousness) and provide the ultimate answers to the riddle of our being and all else.

In psychosynthesis, Jesus is the perfect model for what Roberto Assagioli called *Self-actualization,* as Christ is the perfect model for what he termed *Self-Realization.* The Holy Name of Jesus Christ, which has been consecrated and built into a tremendous Word of Power in the psychic atmosphere of the Earth, can help us accomplish the following things:

1. Help us to cast out devils, in ourselves, in a given locale, and in others.
2. Help us speak in new tongues.
3. Help us to heal the sick—ourselves and others.
4. Help us to receive whatever we ask in His Name (with FAITH).
5. Help us and others to achieve Salvation.
6. Help us find and penetrate into the Inner church, the Brotherhood of the Rosy Cross.

What do these things really mean? Very briefly, they can be interpreted as follows:

a. To cast out devils is to transform negative thoughts

and feelings into positive and balanced ones; to change our state of consciousness; and to perform a true alchemical operation of raising the lower into the higher, and transmuting vices into virtues.

b. To speak in new tongues is to transform, to expand our state of consciousness so that we can know, understand, and do things which we could not do before.

c. To heal the sick is to apply the panacea; the Divine Light in a higher state of consciousness to heal physical, emotional, and mental diseases and spiritual blindness.

d. To ask in His Name and to receive what we asked for is to know what we should do and strive for, in the light of higher states of consciousness, and to have the strength to actually do it.

e. To achieve Salvation is to attain true spiritual Initiation or Illumination.

f. To find and to penetrate into the Inner church or the Brotherhood of the Rosy Cross is to raise one's level of consciousness and vibratory level so that one can communicate in "thought" with true Masters and Adepts and enter with one's Inner Bodies, into the *Temple of Wisdom* in the Inner Planes.

The central reason why the Holy Name of Jesus Christ can perform these "transformations of human consciousness" and "miracles" is that this Holy Name, when vibrated with FAITH, focuses our whole attention upon the divine in us and in the world; it stimulates into activity key psychospiritual Centers; it blazes open a channel and a "sympathetic rapport" between our superconscious and our conscious; and that it raises the vibratory level of our human consciousness to that of the spiritual realms.

It accomplishes this through a synthesis of human effort rising from below and of Divine Grace flowing down from above; through a psychospiritual process involving all of man's higher human faculties and his male-female polarities; and through the peculiar law that "like attracts like", and that man can only comprehend and draw that which is outside and above him by what is in him. As an advanced student of the Mysteries put it:

> The beginning of the practice of the Holy Name is our intense faith in the Lord as our personal Healer and Savior. All that really separates us from receiving deliverance through the Holy Name in all our tribulations is but our lack of faith. It is at the point where Living Faith and the dawning of the true knowledge of God appear in the student's consciousness that the Holy Name will bring peace, victory, and deliverance when the latter is tempted, exhausted, nervous, irritable, angry, worried, confused, or "led astray". A heart filled with the Light and Presence of the Name will not tolerate any negative thoughts, images, feelings, and desires; and should these come, they will be instantly repelled or transmuted as light dispells and transforms darkness. The Aura of the student then acts as a steel "armour", the armour of Light of the Soul filled with the Divine Light of God.*

In the words of a real Alchemist and Qabalist I once knew:

> When we say "Jesus is my all," the Light of the world illuminates our whole visible and invisible bodies; the Light generated by the Holy Name is actually He, Himself. He heals our spiritual blindness, expels our impurities, purifies our spiritual leprosy and raises the dead and sleeping powers within us into living forces. He is now crucified in us. He dies and is gloriously resurrected as conqueror within us. Afterwards, His personality lives in us and instructs us in the exalted Mysteries until he has made us complete and ready for perfect regeneration— when He mounts to heaven to send us from thence the Spirit of Truth. It is at this point, our attainment of the lowest grade of the true Adeptship of the Spirit, that the sublime Rosicrucian axiom "Jesus is my all" becomes a living fact for us . . . It is the theurgic thought-power of the words "is my all" which causes His Light to spread all over the visible and invisible anatomy of man, tracing a Cross of Light, and bringing real and vast alchemical changes in us. †

Finally, the Name is also a passport, a key, or

---

*SRIA Documents
† SRIA Documents

door to the rich pastures of the Inner Church, the Communion of Saints, and the Brotherhood of the Rosy Cross. As Jesus stated: "When two or three of you are gathered together in My Name, there shall I be in the midst of you."

A true Initiate, whenever he pronounces the Holy Name, feels to be in communion with all the Holy Ones and the Celestial Hierarchies who labor for the spiritual progress of mankind. Thus, he adopts the "Way of the Name" as the best method of establishing conscious contact with the Holy Ones, with all those he loves, near or far, "dead" or alive.

In conclusion, I can say that the Holy name is the simplest and most effective method to obtain actual contact with God, and with the Divine Spark within ourselves.

This contact and union is the ultimate and most coveted goal towards which all the most profound and arcane Mysteries of Mankind converge as into a center. In the words of Karl von Eckhartshausen: "Do you wish, man and brother, to acquire the highest Happiness possible? Search for Truth, Wisdom, and Love. But you will not find these except in unity, and this is Jesus Christ, the Anointed of God."*

It is also written: "Without Me, Ye can do nothing." (John 15:5)

A good clue to the deeper meaning of the previous statement can be found in the following metaphor: without a source of light, no man can see anything. To see on the physical plane, it is necessary to have physical light. The same holds true for the spiritual planes which ultimately, control and brought the physical plane into being.

On the spiritual planes, a source of spiritual Light is as necessary as physical light is on the physical planes. This spiritual Light, Life, and Energy by which all things were created, are sustained, and will eventually be perfected, is "Jesus Christ", the Light of the World and of our souls.

---

*Cloud Upon the Sanctuary, p. 85.

"Jesus Christ';', therefore, can be looked upon as light or electricity which are universal and with us always and everywhere. But, like light or electricity, in order that they may be expressed and used in this world, a *vehicle of expression,* a "little Temple", a "light bulb", is absolutely necessary.

The Name of Jesus Christ is just such a light bulb, a "lens", as the Eastern Monk called it, or a vehicle of expression for the reception and manifestation of the Cosmic Principle.

Actually, it is our human consciousness which is the true "light bulb" and "temple" for the Light, Life, and Love of Christ; and His Name is more like a "switch" or a "tuner" that brings the power through. Such a Name must "become flesh" in us and expand in us until our whole personality and human consciousness are permeated by It and become the "light bulb" (the Temple) of the Divine Spark in the world. Only repeated and daily use, with FAITH and reverence, will make this happen.

Chapter Six

THE SIGN OF THE CROSS
ITS NATURE AND USE

The central theme of the Western Spiritual Tradition is that God DWELLS IN MAN and that the only way in which man can ever "find God," have a genuine "experience of the Divine Presence," and achieve "union with God" is to look for Him within the upper reaches of his own being and consciousness. This most important of all spiritual truths was taught by Apostolic Christianity and explicitly stated by some of the Fathers of the Christian Church.

In the Bible, St. Paul in I Cor. 3:16 states: "Know ye not that ye are the Temple of God and that the Spirit of God dwells in you."

St. Paul went as far as specifying that the Spirit of God resides in the Spiritual Body of man and it must be sought there, and not in the physical body. St. Augustine tells us: "Lord, I have sought you in all the temples of the world and lo, I found you within myself." To this he added: "If a man does not find the Lord within himself, he will surely not find Him in the the world."

There are many specific and practical ways by which a sincere and devoted person can come in direct contact with the Lord (i.e. with his own Divine Spark or Spiritual Self) and thus benefit from His Energies, Guidance, and Presence. All the world religions have implicitly or, sometimes, even openly shown their devotees how to bring about this contact, communion, and finally union with the Spiritual Self or Lord.

Likewise, all the genuine Mystery Schools have specific teachings and exercises designed to achieve this union. At the core of both the religious and occult approaches, we find what we have termed the "Seven Fundamentals of the Holy Wisdom" which contain all the necessary theoretical teachings and practical exercises to lead man to a true Spiritual Illumination, which is the result of entering in a *conscious contact* with the "Divine Within".

The first of the Seven Fundamentals is the knowledge and practical use of Divine Names or Names of Power, which we discussed in our previous chapter. The second Fundamental is the SIGN of the CROSS, which is a special application of the use of the Divine Names on the TREE OF LIFE. Before we begin our analysis of the Sign of the Cross and how it operates let us briefly review the nature and use of Words of Power:

1. Names of Power are words, or psychic media, which convey and elicit the various units of human consciousness which we call intuitions, thoughts, feelings, and vital energies.

2. Words are true "bundles of energies" or "streams of focused thought and emotion." They are the lens which direct and focus our whole attention upon a certain object, power, or being. They are the catalysts which convey and elicit certain energies and "states of consciousness" in our Sphere of Sensation or field of consciousness.

3. Names of Power are the pyschospiritual means by which we invoke a certain Presence, induce a certain state of consciousness, and focus our awareness. They are the means through which we create in ourselves (in our imagination or in the Astral Light) an "image" or

"fascimile" of that which is without or above us, and by which the powers and energies that are outside of us can contact us and enter into our Aura.

4. Words are so important to man in all his activities, whether sacred or profane, because they are the means by which he can deliberately awaken and focus his energies, feelings, thoughts, and intuitions by *an effort of the will.*

5. Names of Power are the key regulators and transformers, or "switches" of man's human consciousness and of his inner life. It is through these transformers that all awakening, focusing, and expansion of human consciousness take place.

6. Divine Names have both an outer and an inner part, a "letter" and a "spirit" that gives life to the letter. These parts can be represented by a *chalice* (the form or letter) and by the Light and Life (the force or Spirit) that fills the chalice, for the mind of man takes on the form of the object it beholds and his energies run along the lines traced by the mind and enliven the things about which we think.

7. Names of Power have both a male and female polarity. They are "points of entry" or channels, through which higher energies and levels of consciousness reach us. They are also "projectors" or channels through which we can manifest our energies and consciousness. Hence, they are like a LADDER OF JACOB on which ANGELS are ascending and descending.

8. To make a Word of Power come "alive" in us and become a channel for Spiritual LIGHT and LIFE that will transform our consciousness and then our lives and our being, rather than merely remain another name, abstraction, or sound, three elements are needed:*

---

*One must realize and understand fully and utilize these three elements. THIS CAN NOT BE STRESSED STRONGLY ENOUGH!

To know the Word of Power and some of its basic meanings and correspondences.

To meditate regularly upon it so as to *expand* the set of meanings and associations it has for us, and to relate it to our being and life so as to discover the *personal* message, or correspondences, it contains for us on different levels of consciousness.

To use it with deep FAITH, for ultimately it is FAITH that will connect it with its spirit and which will make it come alive in us and become a LIVING CHANNEL for the Power which it represents.

9. All of the above can be synthesized and expressed in the central formula of the Western Spiritual Tradition upon which we should meditate regularly and check with our own personal experience and results: "By Names and Images are all Powers awakened and re-awakened."

When it comes to the Cross and the many rituals and practical exercises connected with it, the first thing we should do is to suspend, momentarily, our judgement and our associations of ideas and feelings about it being a specifically Christian symbol.* The Cross is a universal symbol which can be found in one form or another, and with different interpretations, in all the world religions and in all the genuine Mystery Schools.

The earnest seeker will find the Cross at the very beginning of his spiritual journey on the very threshold of the Path, just as the true Adept and Saint will "wear it on his breast" as the unmistakeable sign of his spiritual attainment. (It will be shinning in his aura radiating from the Heart Center).

The true disciple will use the Cross and live with it *daily,* learning how to formulate it in his Aura throughout the

---

*The Christian Traditions have openly claimed and used the cross, though in an unconscious manner, and for the most part without the slightest realization of its deeper and more practical implications.

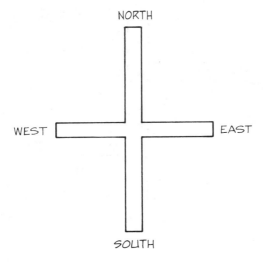

Four Cardinal Points Represented by the Cross.

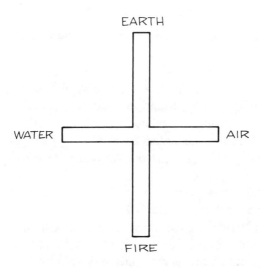

Four Elements Represented by the Cross

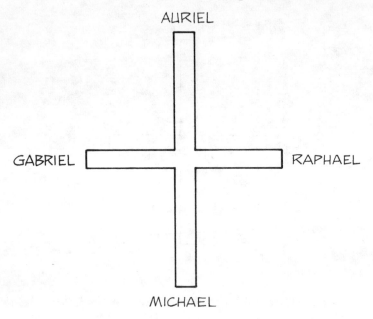

Four Archangels Represented by the Cross.

long journey of his spiritual quest for the union with God.

In the Mystery Schools, the Cross symbol also played a central role and can be found in many forms with different attributions and rituals attached to it. Thus, we have Four Cardinal Points represented by a Cross; Four elements represented by a Cross; and Four Archangels represented by a Cross (See diagrams).

Several practical spiritual exercises are also found to be based on the symbol of the Cross.

Why should the Cross be so important to man and what key functions does it perform? Modern social science is now finally beginning to recognize what the Holy Wisdom has been teaching for ages. Namely, that the essence of man is not his body or his possessions, but rather the LIFE that flows and expresses through his body. This life originates in the Spirit of man, manifests through his psyche, and culminates in its expression through human consciousness.

The essence of man's Self, which flows out his Spirit, is now seen as being *knowledge, love,* and *life,* which proceed from DIVINE WISDOM, DIVINE LOVE, and DIVINE LIFE. The key functions of man's psyche which, taken together, constitute what we call human consciousness are: thinking, feeling, willing, intuition, imagination, biopsychic drives, and sensations. These processes are linked with and seem to express, the three attributes of the Self:

> KNOWLEDGE
> LOVE
> CREATIVE ENERGIES

It is in these terms that man's behavioral expression of speaking and acting are explained and they constitute the central focus of anthropology, sociology, and psychology. To simplify matters, we can say that the essence of man's being is:

> SPIRIT
> SOUL
> BODY

expressing at the ontological level as knowledge, love, life; and at the existential level as thinking, feeling, and willing which express in speech and action, and which manifest at the unconscious, conscious, and superconscious levels.

Religion, philosophy, and science, the three major systems of human knowledge and approaches to Reality, have all expressed and recognized in their own way and words the foregoing. Thus, we can see God as a Trinity: Divine Wisdom, Divine Love, and Divine Creative Energy or Life; and that man should worship God in spirit and in truth (i.e. subjectively and objectively) with all his:

> HEART (FEELINGS)

SOUL (WILLING)
MIND (THINKING)

Philosophy, through the works and expressions of different philosophers has defined man's being or essence as thinking, loving, and creating.

Thus we have:

Descartes: "Cogito ergo sum" I think, therefore, I am, the more I think, the more I am; I do not think, I am not.

Pascal: "Amo ergo sum," I love, therefore, I am; the more I love, the more I am; I love nothing, I am nothing.

W. James: "Acto ergo sum," I do, therefore I am; the more I do, the more I am; I do nothing, I am nothing.

In other words:

1. The essence of man is what he knows, what he loves, and what he does, which consciously expresses the attributes of his spiritual Self through his human self.

2. There is absolutely nothing that man can do in any area of life which does not require some knowledge (awareness), some love (desire), and some life (creative energy). Therefore, the more man knows, loves, and can express himself creatively, the more he is and can act in this world to do whatever he wishes to accomplish.

3. As knowledge, love, and life define both what man is and what man does; and we understand that man is here on Earth to become a fuller, more conscious, and creative being than he was, prior to incarnating here; then the central purpose of his pilgrimage on Earth is to become capable of knowing more, loving more, and creating more: To deepen, expand, and heighten his consciousness so as to live a more

"holy" life which will culminate in the *creation of a new being.*

This is precisely where the Cross in its deeper implications and its practical applications comes in.

Let us briefly analyze five of the major theoretical implications and practical applications of the Cross Ritual:

1. The Cross Ritual as a Means of Consciously Bringing More Spiritual Light and Life to Man:

In the Egyptian religion we can find the most direct and explicitly "exoteric" statement concerning the Cross and its inner and practical meaning. The Egyptians called the Ankh the Sign of Life, the "door" to awakening and renewed spiritual life. The Christians linked it with SALVATION, RESURRECTION, AND REGENERATION. In point of fact, the central purpose of the Cross Ritual is precisely to *awaken* man's spiritual life from its present "sleep" or latency, by *activating certain key centers on the Tree of Life.* It is the most simple, direct, safe, and effective means by which one can shift the "gears" of his consciousness, tap the reservoir of latent spiritual energy that exists within him, and establish a conscious "bridge" or rapport between his conscious and superconscious.

It is through the ritual of the Cross, that the leap is made between the "state of nature" and the "state of grace", between normal and spiritual consciousness, and that the Initiate links with his "contact point", or "switch of power" in the inner worlds.

Therefore, at the beginning of any practical spiritual operation, it is the Sign of the Cross that is used to re-establish and to reaffirm the CROSS of LIGHT within one's Sphere of Sensation by which the Divine Light and Fire are reached and drawn down to suffuse man's entire psychic being. As such the Cross does indeed, as we shall see later, contain the practical keys for the process of Spiritual Regeneration, Spiritual Resurrection, and genuine Spiritual

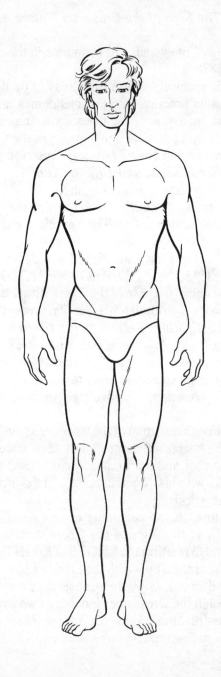

Illumination.

From time immemorial certain bodily "locations" and "organs" have been linked with certain psychological and psychic attributes and expressions, and this has not been by chance or arbitrarily!

Thus, knowledge and thinking have always been associated with the *head;* love and feeling have been associated with the *heart**, and creative energy and life have been associated with man's *hands* and *shoulders.* (See illustration.)

When we remember that man not only has a physical body but also a spiritual body (i.e. the etheric, astral, mental, and spiritual bodies) and that these "bodies" have corresponding "organs" or "centers" of *activity* (called flowers of the Lotus in the East, and Roses in the West), the foregoing will begin to make a lot more sense . . .

Four of the most important Psychospiritual Centers are located precisely around the following areas:

> The CROWN (Primum Mobile) Overshadowing the Head
>
> HARMONY (the Sun) Overshadowing the Heart
>
> MERCY (Jupiter) Overshadowing the Left Shoulder
>
> SEVERITY (Mars) Overshadowing the Right Shoulder

It is through these Centers, and *not their physical counterparts* (head, heart, and shoulders) that knowledge, love, and life, thinking, feeling, and willing manifest themselves.

A Fifth Center, the KINGDOM (the Earth) is also touched and actived as the shaft of Light and Life, descending from the Head into the Heart, is then extended to the feet where this Center is located.

Thus the Spiritual Center (the Head) is connected with the Psychic Center (the Heart), and with the Physical Center (the Feet); GOD, HUMANITY, and NATURE are linked

---

*Note that passion, and the lower emotions are linked with the Solar Plexus.

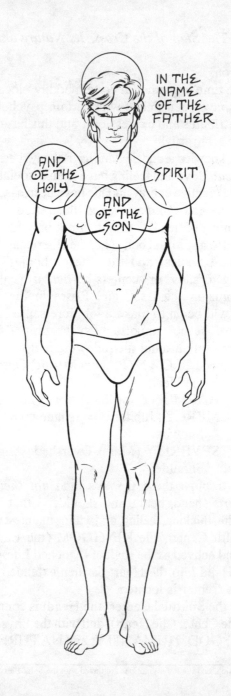

in the inner AXIS MUNDI*, and we become a channel and a transformer for the Energies and the Life of the Spirit to flow through our being to humanity, and to nature. And this brings us to the traditional Sign of the Cross of the Christians.

> Here the devotee touches his forehead with his fingers saying:
> "IN THE NAME OF THE FATHER"
> then he touches his heart with his fingers saying:
> "AND OF THE SON"
> and finally, he touches his right and left shoulders with his fingers saying:
> "AND OF THE HOLY SPIRIT"

What he is doing in fact is directing all his attention and psychic energies, through the help of his physical or astral hand, to his Head Center, Heart Center, and Shoulder Centers, wherein he vibrates these three Divine Names. The reason for doing this should now be obvious: it is to awaken and activate these Centers, to correlate and distribute their various energies, and to suffuse, via the activity of these Centers, his whole Sphere of Sensation with the Light and Fire he is "drawing from on high."

The FATHER here is the symbol of Divine Wisdom, the SON of Divine Love, and the HOLY SPIRIT of Divine Creative Energies. By vibrating these Names of Power with all the "FAITH" he is able to muster in their corresponding Centers, what the devotee is saying from the spiritual standpoint is:

> "Let the Divine Wisdom of God manifest through my Head Center",
> "Let the Divine Love of God manifest through my Heart Center",
> "Let the Divine Creative Energy of God manifest

---

*AXIS MUNDI: the "world shaft" or consciousness continuum flowing from the Spiritual to the Physical Dimension.

through my Shoulder Centers".

To the degree that the devotee is ready for this and in accordance with his FAITH (degree of concentration, knowledge for what he is doing, and love for what he is doing) an immediate transformation and expansion of his thinking activities, of his feelings, and of his vital energies will take place as each Center is activated and correlated with the others. In this way, the Sign of the Cross will serve as a practical exercise to awaken, stimulate, and intensify man's major faculties through which he can express himself. In the words of an advanced spiritual scientist:

> When we say 'In the Name of the Father' and place our fingers on the forehead, we actually point with our fingers to an important organ in our spiritual body just below the space where God dwells in us 'on high'. The vibration set up in motion by our loving thought about our heavenly Father activates the Divine Essence of the 'Crown' which pours into our Heart Center as a veritable though unseen Glory (Shaft of White Light). This activation of the 'Crown' itself is described by St. Peter: 'Ye shall receive a Crown of Glory'. When we say: 'And of the Son' and place our fingers on our heart, we again actually point with our fingers to a space in our spiritual body where the Divine Light, in the words of the Prophet Isaiah poured upon us from 'on high', is activating another spiritual organ suffusing us with the Divine Love of the Son. And when we say: 'And of the Holy Spirit', touching our right and left breast respectively, we activate these spiritual sensoria within us which manifest as the creative and vitalizing power of the Holy Spirit in our lives. Finally when we say: 'Amen' and join our hands together, mentally affirming the presence of the Triune God *within us,* we actually close the spiritual currents within the periphery of our spiritual body in order to maintain this awakening to spiritual awareness as long as possible.*

We can see some of the reasons how St. Paul could say about the Sign of the Cross: "For the preaching of the Cross is to them that perish foolishness; but unto us who are saved, it is the Power of God." Let us keep in mind that the Sign

---

*S.R.I.A. Documents, Bishop Theodotus.

of the Cross is vastly more than the foregoing which merely points to one of its most elementary and important applications!

2. The Sign of the Cross as a Means to Achieve Self-Mastery and True Peace.

In the previous explanation and analysis, we showed how the Sign of the Cross could bring true self-knowledge to Man by awakening spiritual consciousness and linking him with his spiritual Self through the activation of key psycho-spiritual Centers. Now we shall briefly discuss how it is also a practical and effective means to achieve self-mastery and harmony with one's spiritual Self, or in other words a *Spiritual Psychosynthesis!*

Self-mastery can be achieved only when three basic prerequisites exist:

A. When one has gained a *minimum* of self-knowledge and self-understanding.

B. When one's human self is connected, to some degree, with one's spiritual Self which then becomes the Center, or integrating principle, of one's being.

C. When the various planes and energies; one's super-conscious, unconscious, and conscious, are properly correlated and equilibrated so that the Power of the Spirit can express itself through them.

The Sign of the Cross, by awakening spiritual consciousness in one's psyche, accomplished condition'A' (above). By linking the superconscious with the conscious, which opens a channel between them, the Sign of the Cross accomplished condition 'B'. Finally, by setting up an "axis mundi" and an energy distribution pattern from the spiritual to the physical plane, linking intuition, thinking, feeling, and willing, as well as the "subjective dimension with the objective dimension"*, the Sign of the Cross then accom-

---

*Subjective dimension/objective dimenson: the inner and outer worlds; consciousness and action.

plished condition 'C'. In the words of an advanced spiritual scientist:

> History tells us that when emperor Constantine was about to wage a decisive battle with his enemies, there appeared to him in a vision the Sign of the Cross with the message 'In Hoc Signo Vinces' which means *by this sign you will conquer*... If you want to conquer your inner enemies and acquire spiritual rulership over your mortal nature, which is the goal of all true spiritual development, the same Sign of the Cross is this very moment above you. Its message is ever the same 'by this Sign you will conquer.' Yes, take up His Cross as more than a mere 'dead symbol.' Make it a living force in your consciousness, and you will soon experience a foretaste of what St. Paul calls 'the Power of God.'*

3. The Cross as the Model for all Creative Processes, and the Means by Which Man's Higher Self can Express Itself in the World.

One of the most important and fascinating powers that man shares, to a small extent, with God, is the power to create and to bring into being new things. To create anything, man needs three basic ingredients:

1. Knowledge of what man wants. The formulation of an idea or picture of the new reality to be brought about.

2. Love or a strong desire for that particular idea or picture to be realized.

3. The will or energy necessary to realize it and to translate the idea into an objective reality. (We get this energy from our Shoulder Centers while "Feeling" comes from the Heart Center, and "Thinking" comes from the Head Center).

Thus, the creative process involves an *idea* vitalized by *love* which then sets in motion the *energies of the Will* which will bring about its realization. This process is directly related to the Ritual of the Cross, following its exact

---

*SRIA Documents, Bishop Theodotus

sequence. Thus, the knowledge, the ideas and pictures, are "hatched" in the Head Center, the love or desire flows out of the Heart Center, while the energies necessary for its realization are drawn from the Shoulder Center, and their interrelation is brought about by tracing the Sign of the Cross.

To use the Ritual of the Cross as a model for any creative endeavor, the following steps should be followed:

A. The devotee should begin by tracing the Sign of the Cross upon himself to awaken his key faculties and their related Centers by forming a Cross of Light within his Aura.

B. Then the devotee should turn to the "FATHER" with all his FAITH by concentrating in the head region to obtain from Divine Wisdom all the necessary inspiration he needs to formulate and concretize a given ideal or end. He should ask of Divine Wisdom, by continuing his meditation on the Head Center, all the necessary inspiration and knowledge to concretize this idea, or image, which he should visualize vividly.

C. Once this ideal or image, is *clearly* formulated and visualized, the devotee should turn to the "Son" with all his FAITH by concentrating on the heart region, to obtain from Divine Love all the necessary love and desire to "fertilize" that ideal and its representation.

D. Finally, when the devotee feels at one with his ideal and image (once they have been indrawn into him, as it were, from being first objectified from outside of him . . .) he should then turn to the "Holy Spirit" with all his FAITH, by concentrating on the shoulder region, to obtain from the Divine Creative Energies all the willpower, or creative life force, he needs to realize and objectify this ideal in the world through his actions.

E. Should at any time the ideal or its image weaken,

become ambiguous, vague, or confused during the ritual process, the devotee should turn to Divine Wisdom (in the Head Center) to receive fresh inspiration, knowledge, and power to concretize his visualization!

Should his love or desire for this ideal weaken, become ambivalent, or torn between other goals and ends, he should turn again to Divine Love (in the Heart Center) to receive an intensification and deepening of his love and desire for it.

Finally, should his Will or energies become sapped or depleted, or be insufficient for the task at hand, he should then turn again to the Divine Creative energy (in the Shoulder Centers) to receive fresh life forces and a vitalization and strengthening of his will power and resolve to accomplish that end.

4. The Cross as a Means to Awaken and Activate all the Psychospiritual Centers on the Tree of Life and to Eventually Achieve True Spiritual Illumination with God.

Another very important exercise based on the Ritual of the Cross is the *Qabalistic Cross*. This exercise is drawn from the mystical tradition of Israel (hence either Hebrew or English words may be used) which has been adapted and largely used by all legitimate Mystery Schools in the West.

For this exercise, the devotee should begin by breathing deeply a few times, by relaxing physically and mentally, and by preparing himself inwardly. Then he should turn to the SPIRITUAL EAST* and point with his fingers to the Head Center saying:

"A TEH" (For Thine)

Visualizing a shaft of brilliant white light flowing out of his

---

*SPIRITUAL EAST: the HEAD CENTER where the Divine Light resides in the symbolic language of the Sages.

Head Center and directing it with his attention and fingers to his Feet Center saying:

"MALKUTH" (is the Kingdom)

He should feel the Light and the Life of the CROWN flowing down to his feet and awakening his Feet Center with an unmistakable sensation, in so doing, an "axis mundi," a shaft of Light, or psychic channel, will be established from the head to the feet, connecting the superconscious with the conscious and unconscious (Heaven, Earth, and Hell), the spiritual Self with the human self. In so doing, all the Centers on the Middle Pillar will be affected and activated to a certain degee. We can then see that the Spiritual Self will consciously bring its vitalizing energies throughout the devotee's entire being, thus establishing a life current between the two terminal Centers on the Tree of Life, the Spiritual and the Physical, affirming and establishing the rulership of the Divine Spark in the devotee's "little kingdom."

After a living response and awakening has taken place and has been EXPERIENCED by the devotee, and after the Shaft of Light connecting the head and the feet has been firmly established and FELT by him, then the devotee should point his fingers to his right shoulder saying:

"VE GEBURAH" (and the POWER)

to awaken that Center, and trace a horizontal shaft of pink-purple light to his left shoulder where he should vibrate the Name:

"VE GEDULAH" (and the GLORY)

In so doing the devotee will not only bring the Divine Light, Fire, and Life down into his human psyche and consciousness, and affirm the rulership of the Divine Principle in him, but he will also be able to use these energies and inspirations constructively and creatively in his being and his life in a balanced way.

Here, a synthesis will be made between the male and female principles in him, between Severity and Mercy, just as a connection is made between the Spiritual and Physical principles, the crown and the Kingdom, in him (through the vertical Shaft of Light).

Moreover, the integration of Worship (climbing on the "Sacred Mountain" on the vertical axis) and Service (using the Light and Fire received on the "Sacred Mountain" to help and enrich the lives of others on the horizontal axis) will also be brought to consciousness and will be emphasized.

Man's "little kingdom", the billions of cells, entities, energies, and principles that dwell, consciously, unconsciously, and superconsciously in him, do belong to the Spiritual Self who will rule them and synthesize them eventually. The power and the life of man should also be consecrated to the GOD WITHIN and to the completion of the Great Work—*which is what this ritual affirms and temporarily realizes in the devotee!*

This Ritual should then be completed by bringing both hands to touch each other in the center of the devotee's chest, wherein he will vibrate the words:

"LE OLAM AMEN" (So be it)

which closes the circuit of Light and Life within his Sphere of Sensation and which preserves and strengthens the Cross of Light which is glowing in him.

When this exercise is carried out with full consciousness and attention, and with living FAITH, it will temporarily induce a brief glimpse of genuine spiritual Illumination and at-one-ment between the Spiritual Self and the human self, thus giving him a foretaste of what will eventually happen to him on a permanent basis and helping him to get a little closer to that great goal.

5. The Cross as a Means to Integrate Reality Within Oneself; God with Humanity and Nature, and the Inner

World with the Outer World.

The Sign of the Cross is also the means by which the devotee can establish a true *axis mundi* within himself (a shaft of Light or Energy connecting the superconscious, the conscious, and the unconscious) through which all levels of reality and all Powers can be contacted and linked with each other:

> The Spirit of God through the awakened Head Center,
> Humanity through the Heart Center,
> Nature or the body through the Feet Center.

In this ritual, God the Father, Nature the Mother, and Humanity the Son, are invoked and synthesized in the consciousness of the devotee, and the inner work is correlated with the outer work.

The higher Energies of the Spirit (Divine Light, Fire, and Life) are brought from the head to the heart where they are radiated to Humanity, and from the heart to the feet where they are radiated to Nature, thus linking the subjective world of the devotee (his Sphere of Sensation and field of consciousness) with the objective world of Humanity and Nature.

There are many other special applications and variants of the Ritual of the Cross, just as there are many more correspondences, meanings, and treasures connected with it on different Planes of Being and states of consciousness. But these will have to be discovered by the devotee himself, through his own *personal experience* and exploration of them. Enough has been said in this chapter to launch a sincere seeker and to guide him on his way to this personal discovery.

It has been said that "the mystery of life is not a problem to be solved but a Reality to be experienced." Likewise, the secrets and treasures of the Cross Ritual are not abstractions to be discussed or written about, but Powers and Realities to be directly and personally experienced!

Chapter Seven

THE LORD'S PRAYER: ITS NATURE AND USE

In this chapter, we shall look briefly at the nature and practical use of the Lord's Prayer so as to make it come 'alive' within the consciousness and life of the devotee.

Please bear in mind that my purpose is not to tell you what it is; that you will have to discover for yourself from personal experience. My aim is to increase your reverence and appreciation of it, and to motivate you to use it frequently with some understanding of its function and practical applications, so it may reveal its mysteries and treasures to you as it has to me.

The Nature of the Lord's Prayer (what it is):

The Lord's Prayer is an interrelated set of symbols, or formulae, containing both knowledge about man's psychospiritual anatomy and an integrated set of practical exercises designed to awaken Man's psychospiritual Centers, train key human and spiritual faculties, "nourish" his entire pyschospiritual nature, and achieve Spiritual Illumination or union with the Divine Spark or the Spiritual Self.

The Functions of the Lord's Prayer (how it operates):

The Lord's Prayer must be activated in man's field of

consciousness; but from there it can also function in the subconscious and the superconscious mind through its language of images and archetypes. The key faculty that makes the Lord's Prayer effective and "living" is FAITH*, as it is for any other ritual.

The Purpose of the Lord's Prayer (what it can do):

The Lord's Prayer has many purposes operating on different levels. Here are some of the major ones:

1. *Psychologically:* it can be used to awaken man at the psychological level, to focus his attention and the various functions of his psyche upon whatever he is about to undertake.

2. *Socially:* it can be used to unite the thoughts, feelings, and energies of a group of people to achieve social integration and an 'interpersonal psycho-synthesis'.

3. *Spiritually:* it can accomplish many things, chief of which are:
   a. Provide man with a living source of knowledge.
   b. Enable man to train and exercise various psychological and spiritual faculties and thus to develop them.
   c. Progressively awaken, activate, and integrate all the psychospiritual Centers.
   d. Establish a genuine breakthrough of the superconscious into the conscious and open up a channel between the human and the Spiritual Self through which inspirations and energies can flow.
   e. Feed and correlate all of Man's "bodies" (spiritual, mental, emotional, and etheric) and their key faculties.

---

*FAITH: The focused trinity of Thinking, Feeling, and Willing, pouring all of our Knowledge, Love, and Creative Energies upon a given subject.

f. Progressively enable man to link his will with the Will of the Divine Spark within him, so that the latter may manifest Itself in the world, and express in the world attributes of the spiritual Self—Divine Wisdom, Love, and Life.

g. Provide a SAFE and effective way of coming in contact with the Inner Worlds, the Celestial Hierarchies, and the Brotherhood of the Rosy Cross.

h. Eventually achieve spiritual Illumination and union with the Spiritual Self, which is the goal of human evolution and the highest aim of all genuine spiritual training. As this union of man's conscious self, or ego, with the Spiritual Self, or the Divine Spark, is accomplished in slow degrees by consciously and actively pursuing it, his whole being will come to life and he will lead an increasingly more conscious, creative, useful, and happy life.

How to use the Lord's Prayer:

The Lord's Prayer can be used by oneself or in a group. To use it one should relax, breathe deeply, use the Ritual of the Cross, and then begin. Basically, the Lord's Prayer can be used for four concrete and specific objectives:

1. To develop key human faculties: concentration, visualization, adoration, coordination and balance, and psychosocial integration.

2. To practice meditation and contemplation and thereby expand one's knowledge of its key meanings, correspondences, and applications and of one's psychospiritual anatomy and physiology.

3. It can be used theurgically as a key ritual, bringing Light, Life, and Fire, and a transformer of consciousness and energies; also to link aspiration and inspiration,

invocation and evocation.

4. To practice, construct, and project a major set of thoughtforms which can become a vital and magnetic center in one's being and life, and in that of others. Thus one can:

a. Concentrate and meditate on each key symbol of the Lord's Prayer and then contemplate and experience its "awakening and response" in one's consciousness.

b. Concentrate and meditate on each petition of the Lord's Prayer and then contemplate and experience its impact on each Center of the Tree of Life, and on each "body" and "level of consciousness".

c. Concentrate and meditate on the whole prayer and then contemplate and experience its impact upon one's whole being, consciousness, and daily life.

Key work in meditating on the Lord's Prayer and deciphering its basic meanings, correspondences, and applications, with the idea that "The Kingdom of Heaven is Within You . . ."

Text of the Prayer:

Our Father who art in Heaven;
Hallowed by Thy Name;
Thy Kingdom come;
Thy Will be done on Earth as it is in Heaven;
Give us this day our daily bread, and forgive us our trespasses, as we forgive those who trespass against us;
And lead us not into temptation but deliver us from evil (the Evil One).
Amen.

1. Our Father who art in Heaven;

a. Key symbols: Our, Father, Heaven.

Father: The "Father" is the creative and life sustaining principle, the spiritual principle whence we came, which sustains our lives while here, and to which we shall eventually return in full consciousness.

The "Father" is the real, immortal, spiritual, but as yet unknown Self; it is the Divine Spark, the Christ-Within, Osiris, Atman, the Lord, or whatever the God-in-man is called.

Heaven: It is a higher and qualitatively different state of consciousness than the one we are normally functioning in; it is spiritual consciousness or the superconsciousness.

Our: We all come from the same spiritual Source, are made of the same spiritual Essence, and will eventually achieve the same union with the Spiritual Self. This symbol implies the Fatherhood of God and the Brotherhood of man, and affirms that the Spiritual Self is One and at-one with the same cosmic principle.

b. As a whole, this petition focuses our consciousness upon our Divine Spark, opening up a channel through which the Divine Light and the Spiritual Energies can flow into our whole aura; and it establishes a breakthrough of the superconsciousness into the consciousness. In so doing, we 'Light up the Lamp on high' or "put on our Crown" i.e. we activate Kether. This is the key "switch" by which the Initiate turns on his 'contacts' and the disciple contacts his latent spiritual energy and will that lie dormant within himself.

c. This petition thus leads us to the realization of God's Presence within our being and in the world; it blazes open a psychic channel or "Ladder of Jacob" through which we can rise to Him and enable His Wisdom, Love, and Life to express themselves in our being, in our lives, and in the world.

2. *Hallowed be Thy Name;*
 a. Key symbols: Hallowed be, Thy Name.
   Hallowed be: Implies to become aware of, to enter into a proper relationship with, and to give and take what is appropriate.
   Thy Name: Thy Presence, Consciousness, and Energies of the Divine Spark. A name is a representation of, and a path to, the reality that it represents; in this case, the spiritual Self.

 b. This petition reaffirms and deepens the breakthrough of the superconscious into the conscious established by the first petition, and it draws down the Divine Light and Fire by one's hunger for it and devotion to it.
   While with the help of the first petition we climbed onto the "Sacred Mountain" of consciousness to the place where the Divine Light and Presence dwell; with the present petition we *draw down* and "bring back" that Light and Presence into the field of consciousness, and we suffuse our whole being with It (i.e. our spiritual, mental, emotional, and etheric 'bodies').

 c. This petition formulates a *Cross of Light* in our Aura, distributing and spreading the Light and Energies, and thus the consciousness of the Divine Spark in all the dimensions, nooks, and crannies of our being. Likewise, it also helps every "body", principle, and subpersonality in our being to become aware of, and enter into, a proper relationship with the down-pouring Light of the Spiritual Self. It awakens Chokman and Binah, thus slowly bringing His Consciousness and Presence in our field of consciousness and life, purifying, sanctifying, and perfecting both the human Temple and the world.

3. *Thy Kingdom come;*

a. Key symbols: Thy, Kingdom, Come.

Kingdom: This symbol literally means a king ruling over a body of men occupying a certain territory which is governed by certain laws.

In this petition, the 'kingdom' is our personality with its functions, faculties, energies, and many entities. Thus far, the King (the Divine Spark) is not ruling yet, or is ruling only in an indirect and partial way. The reason that the Divine Spark is not ruling our personality is that the channel between the superconscious and the conscious is not fully developed and operative, the connection between the human and spiritual Self is tenuous, the personality itself is not completed or well coordinated, and many other principles are still ruling our being and lives.

Thy: Refers to the Divine Spark, the Spiritual Self.

Come: Let that come into being, be realized in our life. That is, let the Spiritual Self become the King, Lord, or synthesizing principle of our personality and life.

b. This petition again draws down the Divine Light and Energies of the spiritual Self in a Cross-like fashion, activating *Chesed* and bringing the awareness of the Presence and Rulership of the Divine Spark in all levels of consciousness and aspects of our being.

c. This petition also helps us to realize and to experience that the "Kingdom of God" is a state of consciousness which must be realized within oneself and which will then radiate into, and transform our personal, professional, social, and spiritual life.

It makes us aware that this is the greatest goal and treasure we can and must achieve here on Earth, and it brings with this awareness the strength to realize it, little by little.

4. *Thy Will be done, on Earth as it is in Heaven;*

   a. Key symbols: Thy Will, be done, Earth, Heaven.
Thy Will: The will or focused energies of the Divine Spark.
Be done: Accomplished, translated from potentiality into actuality, brought from the level of an idea to that of an experience, and realized in our being.
Earth: Our field of consciousness, our conscious mind, our personality and our body.
Heaven: The superconscious, the higher levels of consciousness, or spiritual consciousness, where one truly knows oneself, God, one's fellow man, and one's purpose on Earth.

   b. This petition, through another outpouring of spiritual Light and Energies, continues and objectifies the process begun by the former petition.

If God's Kingdom is to be realized in our being, in our lives, and finally in the world, *His Will* must be realized.

God's Will (the Will of the Divine Spark) is always being accomplished in the superconscious, in the spiritual nature of man, but not in his personality (his conscious mind). What takes place at the superconscious and spiritual levels must now be extended and realized at the conscious and personality level.

Once God's Presence has become conscious in us,

His creative Energies or Will can gradually become operative in our personality and life.

The thought form contained in this petition is designed to have us focus on this operation so as to realize it *consciously.*

c. In a third down-pouring of Light and Life through the great Cross of the Tree, Geburah is now activated and energized; Intuition, the flow of spiritual consciousness and Energies, now fuses with our aspirations, thoughts, and feelings, spiritualizing them and thus transforming our words and actions. "Be done" here refers to the transmission and transformation of the Divine Light through the various "bodies" (from the spiritual to the mental, from the mental to the emotional, from the emotional to the etheric and physical) to accomplish the purpose of the Spiritual Self.

It is also the theurgic formula to actually bring the Light and Energies of the Divine Spark from Heaven to Earth, from the Spirit to matter, from Kether to Malkuth.

5. *Give us this day our daily bread;*

a. Key symbols: Give us, this day, daily bread.

Give us: Suffuse our being (Aura and Tree of Life) and let us become aware of these higher Energies.

This Day: Now; wherever we happen to be; the present cycle in our evolution.

Daily Bread: On the *horizontal* axis, the daily bread of our soul is *experience,* on the *vertical* axis it is the *Divine Light.*

b. Every day, in every cycle, at every moment in our lives, the Divine Spark gives us the "daily bread" of our soul, (human experience) but we are not aware of this; we do not understand what is happening to us, or why we are living through the present situation, and therefore, we cannot appreciate it and assimilate it fully.

On the vertical axis, this petition theurically brings down the Divine Light into the Tree of Life and our field of consciousness so as to make us understand our daily experience, be able to assimilate it more fully, and learn the lessons that it brings to us, and thus be grateful to God for it—to receive it and accept it as a gift of God and an opportunity for our human and spiritual growth.

c.   This petition, through a fourth down-pouring of Light and Energy via the Cross of the Tree, activates Tiphareth and makes us more "alive" and aware of the great gift that life and its countless daily experiences truly are. It makes us aware of the myriad opportunities that come our way to learn, to grow, to serve others and thus to live more consciously, creatively, and joyfully.

d.   The thought-form contained in this petition opens up our consciousness and receptivity to the Divine Light coming from on high and to the world around us and thus helps us to become more alive, responsive, and coordinated as a *Temple* of Life and consciousness.

6. *Forgive us our trespasses as we forgive those who trespass against us;*

a.   Key symbols: Forgive us, trespasses, we forgive.
Forgive us: The Spiritual Self always forgives us our trespasses and transforms our errors and mistakes into experiences and lessons that ultimately will benefit us and enable us to mature, to improve, and to transform our imperfections. (But most of the time,

we are unaware of this.)

We forgive: It is we, who many times, do not forgive others, and therefore, ourselves, and live with a heavy burden of anger, resentment, and lowered vibrations.

Trespasses: These imply the violation of physical, psychological, social, and spiritual laws, in deeds, words, emotions, thoughts, or aspirations.

b. This petition makes us aware of a most important universal law: that of action and reaction, or cause and effect, Karma, which takes place on three levels:

1. Between the superconscious and the conscious mind; the spiritual and human self; as well as the conscious and unconscious mind.

2. Between our state of consciousness and our deeds, between our thoughts and our actions.

3. Between ourselves and the world, which includes other human beings, animals, and nature; between the subjective and objective dimensions of life.

c. This petition shows us that what we do unto others, ultimately, we do unto ourselves; that any objective action in the world is immediately followed by a reaction in our consciousness and personality. It shows us, therefore, that as we forgive others we forgive ourselves, and thus become aware that the Divine Spark ("God") has forgiven us.

In this life we constantly violate a number of physical, psychological, social, and spiritual laws, some of which we are aware of, some that we could have obeyed, and others which, at our point in evolution and with our present level of consciousness, we could not have obeyed as yet. Thus, we are much in need of forgiving and being forgiven.

This is the reason why Jesus admonished His

Disciples "forgive them their trespasses not seven times, but 70 times seven times."

d. True forgiveness implies a great deal more than simply saying "I forgive you let us begin anew in a different frame of mind." It implies mental understanding, emotional release, behavioral acceptance, and spiritual 'connection' and perspective. It involves "unclogging" psychospiritual Centers, transmuting many thoughts, emotions, and energies, and actually changing our state of mind. It involves dissolving unbalanced forces, negative thoughts and emotions in our Aura and then in that of others who come to us with their problems and resentments. It means actually transforming vices into virtues and thus performing a genuine alchemical operation in ourselves and then in others.

e. This is made possible by a fifth outpouring of Spiritual Light and Energies which pour out and spread through the Cross on the Tree and focus this time upon Netzach, awakening and activating it.
In its wake, this further outpouring of Spiritual Light and Energies brings a playfulness, a lightness, an acceptance and tolerance which are not weakness or unconcern, but a larger perspective on things, which is unmistakable by the joyfulness and exhuberance they make possible in he who has truly forgiven himself and others.

7. *Lead us not into temptation but deliver us from evil (the Evil One);*

a. Key symbols: Lead us not; temptation; deliver us; evil (one).
Lead us not: Make us aware of, recognize, and be grateful for . . . temptations.

Temptation: The inevitable tests and trials of life we must all face.

Deliver us: Give us the awareness, understanding, and strength to overcome temptations when they come to us and learn the lessons which they contain.

Evil (one): This refers to our lower self, the unbalanced forces, negative thoughts, emotions, and energies in our being which must be conquered and eventually transformed into a pure vehicle for the Higher Self.

b. Of all the petitions of the Lord's Prayer, this is the one that is most apt to be misunderstood, probably because of a poor translation of the original words and meanings.

The spiritual Self never leads us into temptation; it is our lower self, and our conscious self, which does this.

Temptations, moreover, abound in life and are necessary for our human and spiritual growth! The key here is to be aware that a temptation is a *test* sent for our benefit, and to have the wisdom and the strength to resist it and thus pass this test successfully. *Temptations are myriad and of many different types.* Some are physical while others are emotional, mental, and even spiritual; some are within our power to resist, others are not, and can only be overcome with spiritual assistance.

c. This petition is an invocation of the Spiritual Light to help us recognize temptations for what they are, and to have the strength to withstand their onslaught, and the wisdom to be grateful for them. Basically, there are two types of temptations: those created by our lower self (the great majority) and those sent to us by God as a test and our next lesson on the Path (which are still fairly rare for the majority of people).

   d. This petition, through a sixth downpouring of the Spiritual Light and Energies (via the Cross on the Tree of Life), activates Hod and Yesod respectively and gives us the awareness, perspective, and strength to overcome the dark side of our nature, the "shadow" or personal "Devil" which is made up of the accretion of all our vices, wrong deeds, and negative thoughts, emotions, and energies accumulated and crystallized over a long period of time.

8. *For Thine is the Kingdom, and the Power, and the Glory, of the Father and of the Son, and of the Holy Spirit.*

Though some churches do not use this ascription as part of the Lord's Prayer, or omit it altogether, from the esoteric viewpoint it is an integral part of it; it is its very conclusion and culmination.

   a. Key symbols: For Thine, Kingdom, Power, Glory, Father, Son, Holy Spirit.

   For Thine: The Kingdom, ultimately, is of and for the Divine Spark.

   Kingdom: Man's conscious mind, personality, Malkuth.

   Power: Refers here to certain spiritual Energies activated in Geburah and expressing the Will and Justice of God.

   Glory: Refers here to other spiritual Energies activated in Chesed or Gedulah, expressing the Love and Mercy of God.

   Father, Son, and *Holy Spirit:* These are the Trinity, One in essence and threefold in manifestation, i.e. the Divine Light expressing as Divine Wisdom, Love and Creative Energy or Will.

b. This petition is both the culmination and the completion of the Lord's Prayer, and the *Christian version* of the Qabalistic Cross. As the Lord's Prayer began with the Cross Ritual, so it ends with it.

c. This petition now 'fixes' the Cross of Light, which has been awakened and formed through successive downpourings of Light and which has activated all the psychospiritual Centers upon the Aura of the devotee who now "wears it on his breast . . . when he has become a true Initiate.

d. This petition also states in symbols and builds up a final thoughtform, asserting that the Kingdom and its Powers (man's conscious mind, personality, life, and the functions of his psyche) are of, and for, the Spiritual Self to become conscious of Itself, and to manifest Its attributes of Divine Wisdom, Divine Love, and Divine Creative Energies in man and in the world.

e. Having gone down the entire Tree of Life through the *"Path of the Flaming Sword,"* this seventh and final down-pouring of spiritual Light and Energy now focuses upon Malkuth, awakening it, activating it, and dedicating it to the work of the Divine Spark which it must reflect and perform in this world.
    It also opens up the *"Path of the Sword,"* or the Path of return, through which our daily experiences and lessons can be assimilated by our soul and our spiritual Self.

In conclusion, we have seen how the Lord's Prayer contains a true philosophy of Man, God, and Nature; and a practical art, or set of exercises, to awaken, activate, and nourish all of man's "bodies", all of the psychospiritual

"OUR FATHER WHO ART IN HEAVEN"

With this petition we focus our consciousness upon our Divine Spark, opening up a channel through which the Divine Light and Spiritual Energies can flow into our whole Aura.

We are trying to establish a breakthrough of the superconscious into the conscious.

This petition will lead us to the realization of God's Presence within our being and within the world; it blazes open a psychic channel or "Ladder of Jacob" through which we can raise our consciousness up to the Divine Within and enable His Wisdom, Love, and Life to express itself in our being and in the world.

We should be able to visualize and experience a brilliant white light and warmth in the region of our Head Center.

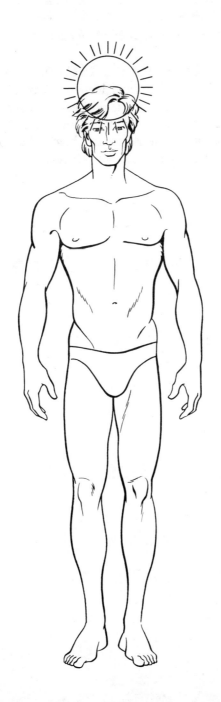

"HALLOWED BE THY NAME"

This petition reaffirms and deepens the breakthrough of the superconscious into our field of consciousness.

In this petition we are "bringing down" the Divine Light and Fire into our whole Aura and being. The process of bringing down this Light and Fire is fueled by our Devotion and Love for it.

This petition formulates a "Cross of Light" in our Aura, as it spreads the Light and Energies throughout our whole being.

It awakens Chokma and Binah, thus purifying our "living Temple."

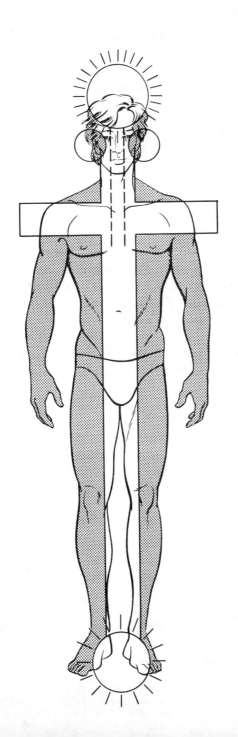

"THY KINGDOM COME"

For a second time we draw down the Light and Energies from the Spiritual Self into our Field of Consciousness in a Cross-like fashion.

This time we are activating Chesed and bringing the presence and rulership of the Divine Spark into all levels of our being.

This petition also helps us to realize the "Kingdom of God" as a state of consciousness within ourselves to radiate and transform our personal, social, and spiritual lives. It makes us aware that the "Kingdom of God" is the greatest goal we can achieve on Earth.

When activating Chesed we should feel the warmth and creative Energies of the Holy Spirit, as we visualize the color Blue.

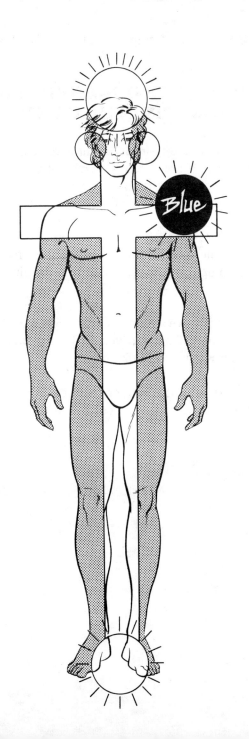

"THY WILL BE DONE, ONE EARTH AS IT IS IN HEAVEN"

A third time are Spiritual Light and Energies brought down; this time we are to activate Geburah and the "Will of God". This petition is designed to focus our will and to consciously realize this operation in our lives.

INTUITION or the flow of Spiritual Consciousness and Energies now fuses with our aspirations, thoughts and feelings, spiritualizing them and thus transforming our words and deeds.

Theurgically, we are bringing the Light and Energies of the Divine Spark from Heaven to Earth, from Spirit to Matter, from Kether to Malkuth.

When vibrating this petition focus the Will and creative Energies as you visualize the color Red around the Right Shoulder Center.

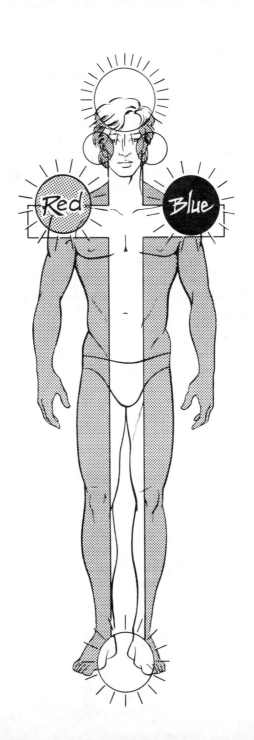

"GIVE US THIS DAY OUR DAILY BREAD"

This petition through a fourth down-pouring of Light and Energy via the Cross of the Tree, activates Tiphareth and makes us more "alive" and aware of the great gift that life and its countless daily experiences that truly are; it helps us to understand and assimilate our daily experiences as lessons brought to us by our Divine Spark and to be grateful to God for them.

With this fourth down-pouring of Light we should visualize our Heart Center opening up with a warm pink glow; we should feel the Higher Emotions and devotion fill and energize.

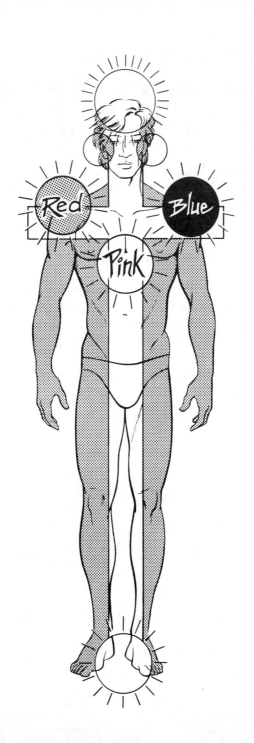

"FORGIVE US OUR TRESPASSES AS WE FORGIVE THOSE WHO TRESPASS AGAINST US"

This fifth down-pouring of Spiritual Light and Energies which diffuse through the Cross on the Inner Tree and focus this time on Netzach, awakening and activating it.

In its wake this further outpouring of the Spiritual Light and Energies brings a playfulness, an acceptance and tolerance which are in fact a view of the larger perspective of things.

What we are trying to accomplish is an "unclogging" of our psychospiritual Centers. We can achieve this goal by dissolving unbalanced forces, negative thoughts and emotions in our own Aura, and then in those who come to us for healing.

When we activate this Center we should feel a sense of unselfishness and emotional heightening, while we are visualizing the color green.

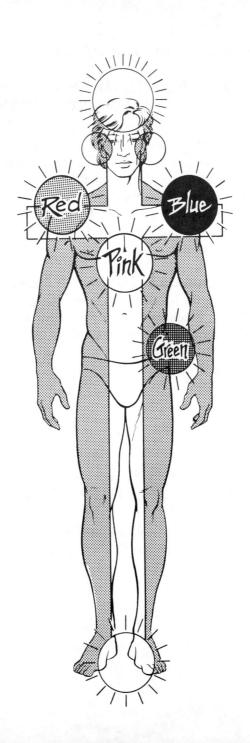

"LEAD US NOT INTO TEMPTATION, BUT DELIVER US FROM EVIL"

The key to this petition is to be aware that the spiritual self does not "lead" us into temptation, but our conscious self does; and to understand that temptations should be looked upon as 'tests' for our Spiritual growth.

In this petition we are invoking the spiritual Light to help us recognize temptations for what they are and to help us withstand their onslaught.

This petition brings down a sixth down-pouring of Light and Energies via the Cross on the Tree of Life, and activates Hod and Yesod, which we are asking to receive the awareness and strength to overcome the dark side of our nature.

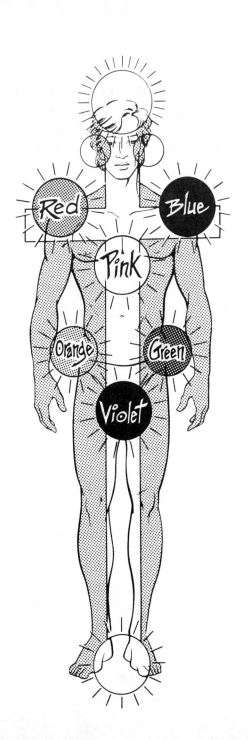

"FOR THINE IS THE KINGDOM, AND THE POWER, AND THE GLORY, OF THE FATHER AND THE SON AND THE HOLY SPIRIT"

This petition completes the Lord's Prayer with a seventh and final down-pouring of Light and Energies.

We are asserting in this petition that the Divine Light, Divine Life, and Divine Energies are to become alive in our Field of Consciousness and in the World.

At this final stage we are focusing all of our knowledge, love, and will on Malkuth, awakening it, activating it, and dedicating it to the work of the Divine Spark.

We are also opening up a path for our daily experiences to be assimilated by our soul and spiritual Self.

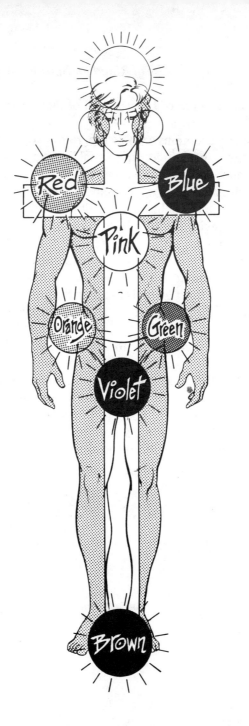

Centers on the Tree of Life, and all of the functions of the psyche.

As such, it contains a whole program of spiritual science in a nutshell, having its functional equivalents in other religions and traditions, and containing all the knowledge and exercises necessary for man to reach true spiritual Initiation: the union of his human self with his Spiritual Self, and then achieving genuine Illumination.

The Initiates of Ancient Greece claimed, in their Mystery Tradition, that Divinity is entombed in nature, that It sleeps spellbound in man, and that man's greatest and highest labor here on Earth is to break that spell and to open that tomb so that the Divine can reawaken and manifest consciously Its attributes in Creation. The Lord's Prayer is, therefore, the practical key to accomplish this Herculean labor. But, as the Lord's Prayer is made living and effective by man's Faith, and as it reflects his level of evolution and consciousness in how it is used and interpreted, man will probably have to use it thousands of times before its true import and practical effects can be discerned and used efficiently with the desired results.

Chapter Eight

THE NICENE CREED: ITS NATURE AND USE

In most Christian Liturgies, the Nicene Creed is preceded by the proclamation: "Wisdom! Stand up! Hear ye the symbol of our holy Faith."

This proclamation points out to those who are spiritually awakened what the Creed truly is and what our attitude towards it should be.

The Nicene Creed contains both the essence of the Christian Faith and the key principles of the Holy Wisdom or Primordial Tradition.

It tells us in symbols what we can find out for ourselves, through our own experiences in the higher states of consciousness. It points to the most important truths concerning Reality, both in Man and in the world; concerning the nature of God and Man, the Divine Spark, the soul and the Church; it tells us about what we are, why we are here, and what we shall become.

As such, the Nicene Creed deals with the most important questions man can ask about himself and reality, and it acts as a *symbolic blueprint* for the interrelationship of God, Humanity, and all of Creation, letting the devotee find a way to:

1. Focus and bring to his awareness what is most important for him and for his life.
2. Stimulate the higher states of consciousness wherein these truths and principles will be experientially realized and lived.
3. Consciously cooperate with the realization and completion of God's plan for man.

"Stand Up": does not only mean to stand up physically (which is the central position, both in the Mystery Schools and in the Orthodox Church, for approaching the spiritual Powers and opening one's self as fully as possible to the inrushing Light) but also to wake up psychospiritually. In other words, to become conscious that one is engaging in a very important task, to fully concentrate upon it, and to open one's whole being (Tree of Life) to it.

"Hear the Symbol of our Holy Faith": shows explicitly that the Creed is written in symbolic and analogical language, and that it contains the kernel of "our Faith" (the key principles and truths of the Holy Wisdom).

Text of the Prayer:

"I believe in One God the Father Almighty, Maker of Heaven and Earth and of all things visible and invisible.

And in one Lord Jesus Christ, the only begotten Son of God; Begotten of His Father, before all ages, Light of Light; Very God of Very God; Begotten not made; Being of one essence with the Father; By Whom all things were made. Who for us men and for our salvation came down from heaven, and was incarnate by the Holy Ghost and of the Virgin Mary. And became Man.

And was crucified also for us under Pontius Pilate; He suffered and was buried.

And the third day He rose again according to the

Scriptures.

And ascended into Heaven and sitteth on the right hand of the Father.

And He shall come again, with glory to judge both the quick and the dead; Whose Kingdom shall have no end.

And in the Holy Ghost, the Lord, the Giver of Life: Who proceedeth from the Father: Who with the Father and the Son together is worshipped and glorified: Who spake by the Prophets.

And in One Holy Catholic and Apostolic Church.

I acknowledge one baptism for the remission of sins.

I look for the resurrection of the dead.

And the life of the ages to come. Amen."

"I believe in One God the Father almighty, Maker of heaven and Earth and of all things visible and invisible."

This statement declares and reaffirms (re-awakens inwardly) the *experience* of the Cosmic God, the Infinite Ocean of Light Who brought all planes of Creation into being. By re-awakening our belief in (and experience of) the Cosmic God, we automatically enter "in rapport" with Him and extend our consciousness towards Him, thus linking our being and consciousness to the whole of Reality and its ultimate Source and Essence.

"And in one Lord, Jesus Christ, the only begotten Son of God; Begotten of His Father, before all ages, Light of Light; Very God of Very God; Begotten and not made; being of one essence with the Father: By Whom all things were made."

This statement, as do most religious statements, has a hieratic or double meaning: one for the normal, uninitiated man, the other for the spiritually awakened man.

In the written history of the world, it is claimed that Jesus Christ is the One Lord, the Son of God who is One with the Father. While in man (the microcosm) for the Initiate, it shows the nature of the Divine Spark that is our true Self. Our Divine Spark should be our Lord and Ruler, the integrating and unifying principle of our psyche and actions.

It is the Divine Spark which is the only begotten Son of God, unlike our vehicles of expression (spiritual, mental, emotional, and physical) which are created or fashioned by the Divine Spark from the substance and energy of each Plane.

The Divine Spark is "begotten" or emanated from the Divine Spirit. It existed long before the world or man's bodies, matter and energy, time and space, came into being.

The Divine Spark is also essentially spiritual Light, Fire, and Life, as an integral part of the Infinite Ocean of Life that manifests the Spirit.

By thinking about the Divine Spark and Its attributes, the devotee also attunes himself to It and becomes more receptive to Its being, and eventually as his consciousness expands and his life changes he comes to the point where he can experience the reality and life of the Divine Spark within his own being.

In short, this passage helps the devotee to enter "in rapport" with his spiritual Self.

"Who for us men and for our salvation came down from Heaven, and was incarnate by the Holy Ghost and the Virgin Mary. And became Man."

This statement continues the development that was started with the previous one. One the exoteric level, it tells us about the historical Jesus the Christ and His Mission: That Christ came down from the Spiritual Worlds to make possible our salvation; that he was fathered by the Holy Ghost and born of the Theotokus, and that He became Man.

On the esoteric level, it tells us more about our Divine Spark: that It came from the Spiritual Worlds and slowly evolved into our vehicles where It now lies asleep; that It will be born *into our Souls,* and into our human consciousness, which will then experience the dawning of true Spiritual Consciousness by the power of the Holy Spirit; and that it will finally live in us and manifest Its Attributes and Will through our bodies (or other vehicles) as it did in the God-Man Jesus Christ, Who is our prototype and archetype.

"And was crucified also for us under Pontius Pilate; He suffered and was buried."

Jesus the Christ was crucified during the reign of Pontius Pilate. Like other men, He suffered, but He knew why He suffered and was buried.

The Divine Spark in us is also crucified on the *Cross of Matter:* the present level of development and coordination of our bodies and our present state of consciousness does not enable It to express Itself any more than our present social and public consciousness enable a truly inspired man to speak and to act according to the dictates of his higher consciousness and thus "crucify Him."

The Divine Spark is thus buried, entombed, and imprisoned in all of us, and It 'suffers' as it cannot express Itself and manifest Its Will and Attributes through our human temple.

"And the third day He rose again according to the Scriptures."

Exoterically, in the world, Jesus the Christ resurrected, came to life again and left the tomb in the rock where His body was lain. Such is what the New Testament tells us.

Esoterically, however, in our Tree of Life, the Divine Spark and true spiritual consciousness will also be resurrected; they will come to life again and permeate our whole human consciousness when the "third day"* will begin. Such is what

---

*Third Day: genuine spiritual evolution as distinguished from animal and biological evolution, the "first day" or phase, and from the human or psychological evolution, the "second day" or phase.

the unwritten Holy Tradition or *Hagia Sophia,* tells us.

"And ascended into Heaven and sitteth on the right hand of the Father."

Exoterically, we are told by the New Testament that Jesus Christ ascended into Heaven and is now "sitting" on the right hand of the Father.

Esoterically, when the Divine Spark has indrawn into our Soul, and when the spiritual consciousness has dawned, it will link us up consciously with the Universal Spirit (the Father) and with Cosmic Consciousness (the Kingdom of Heaven) which are our true home and state of consciousness.

In other words, when a breakthrough of the superconscious into the conscious occurs, Something (i.e. spiritual Light, Fire, and Life) flows down into the centner of our being and consciousness.

But when It reascends and returns from whence It came, into the superconscious, It will this time elevate our whole being with It and bring the very center of our consciousness and being into the superconscious or spiritual realms.

"And He shall come again, with glory to judge both the quick and the dead; Whose Kingdom shall have no end."

Exoterically, the Scriptures and the tradition of the Church tell us that Jesus Christ will come again during the famous "Judgement Day" to judge all those who are alive and those who are "dead"! And from this point onwards, the Millenium will be here and that His Kingdom shall have no end.

Esoterically, this statement refers again to the Divine Spark in us and to spiritual consciousness.

Spiritual consciousness first appears in a flash and then disappears to reappear when we least expect it. Eventually It will come back with Spiritual Light that will surround our being (with *Glory*).

Then, through the perspective of a heightened spiritual consciousness, we shall look upon all of our actions, words, and decisions, both past and present, in quite a different light than we do in a normal state of consciousness.

It is not an outside God or Power who will judge us, but our own Higher Self, taking the true love of God and of our fellow men, and spiritual growth and progress as Its yardstick.

The "quick and the dead" can be seen as meaning basically two things: the things we did and that we remember and the things we did but do not remember, and the things we did when we were illuminated by spiritual consciousness as well as the things we did in our normal state of consciousness.

"Whose Kingdom shall have no end." When the Divine Spark takes control of our being and of our life, and when spiritual consciousness illuminates our stream of awareness, two things happen:

1. One ceases to live in the past and in the future, to live fully now in the present. One steps outside the track and prison of time to enter the eternal Now.
2. One acquires conscious immortality or a continuity of consciousness which is no longer broken by cycles of birth and death, sleep and waking, and the rapidly narrowing and vanishing band of memory.

"And in the Holy Ghost, the Lord, the Giver of Life: Who proceedeth from the Father: Who with the Father and the Son together is worshipped and glorified: Who spake by the Prophets."

Exoterically, this passage affirms our belief in the Third Person of the Holy Trinity, the Holy Spirit, Who is the Spirit of Truth, the Giver and Ruler of Life, Who proceeds from the Father and is bestowed by the Son and Who, with Them, should be worshipped and glorified.

Finally, it asserts that it is the same Spirit of Truth who inspired and spoke through the countless genuine Prophets of

Humanity.

Esoterically, by affirming the reality of the Holy Spirit and by directing our focused attention to It, this formula "tunes us in" to the Presence and Power of the Holy Spirit, and develops a psychic channel through which It can now manifest and work through our human consciousness. The Holy Spirit is one aspect, or manifestation, of the Universal Spirit or Divine Light. The Universal Spirit, or Divine Light, is One in essence but Three in Expression. This specific expression of the Universal Spirit is the "Giver of Life," the Power that quickens, energizes, and enlivens all It comes in contact with. On the Tree of Life, the Center through which It manifests is Binah in the macrocosm and Yesod in the microcosm. It is Divine Wisdom and Divine Love that beget Divine Life and Divine Creative Energy.

First, we had the religion of the Father through Jehovah, then we had the religion of the Son through Jesus Christ; but now it is the religion of the Holy Spirit that we shall develop and which Jesus promised to us as His greatest gift.

While the religion of the Father and of the Son was essentially a "faith religion," (a non-experiential religion without the personal experience and realization of its truths and tenets) the religion of the Holy Spirit, which is in the process of being born, will be essentially an experimental one—one in which the individual will have a direct and firsthand experience and a personal realization of the truths and promises symbolically represented by the former religion.

The coming religion of the Holy Spirit will be a *Path of Initiation,* leading its devotees to genuine Spiritual Illumination, which also had been foreshadowed and promised by the former. For it is through the quickening and life-giving power of the Holy Spirit that the Tree of Life is lit up, that key psychospiritual Centers are activated therein, and that the higher states of consciousness are brought through.

Like the Power and the Center of the Father and of the

Son, so the Power and the Centers of the Holy Spirit have to be "filled with Light", activated, and brought into proper function into the Sphere of Sensation.

Then, as the Holy Spirit inspired and spoke through Prophets, Initiates, and Adepts of old, so It will now generate a breakthrough of the superconscious into the conscious and It will inspire and speak through us.

"And in One Holy Catholic and Apostolic Church."

Esoterically speaking, this affirmation can be interpreted in quite a different fashion than in its exoteric version. There is indeed One Church or Religion that is truly Holy (truly universal and of which Apostolic Christianity was a external and symbolic representation on Earth).

But this Holy and 'Catholic' Religion, that has existed from the first appearance of man on Earth and which will remain with us till humanity has completed its earthly evolution, has never been institutionalized and fully incarnated on Earth and never will be. For it is the One Source and Trunk from which all organized religions have drawn their deepest insights and their loftiest truths, and always will, but which they will never be able to "monopolize" and to express more than partially and in some aspects.

This religion is no more and no less that the *Inner Church,* the 'Church Triumphant', the Communion of Saints, the true Brotherhood of the Rosy Cross, or the Assembly of the Adepts of the Spirit.

Its deepest sanctuaries are the *hearts* and *human consciousness* of the true Mystics and Initiates who walk the Earth. Its symbols and external manifestations can be found in *all* the great world religions.

This Religion is the true and living repository of the Primordial Tradition or the Hagia Sophia. Its major symbol or image is that given by Jesus when He said to Peter:

"And thou art Peter, and on this rock I shall build My

Church."

Peter when asked by Jesus, "Who am I?" has answered:

"Thou art the Christ, the Son of the Living God."

What transpired here is the following: it was the Divine Spark in Peter which enabled him to recognize the Divine Spark or divinity of "Jesus". Jesus in turn, affirmed that His Living Church would be made up of all human beings in whom the Divine Spark had been awakened and who, via the break-through of the superconscious into the conscious, can recognize the Living God in others and in the world, (that is, of true Initiates and spiritually awakened human beings).

"I acknowledge one baptism for the remission of sins."

Exoterically, this passage means that only the "Baptism" of the Christian Faith and, sometimes of even only one Christian church, is valid to wash away one's sins!

Esoterically, there is but one "Baptism" or opening of a key psychospiritual Center, purification of the Aura, and transformation of human consciousness through the opening of a channel by which spiritual energies can flow into our psyche, and that is the downpouring of spiritual Light in response to a deep need of the human heart when man is ready for it.

"I look for the resurrection of the dead."

Exoterically, this was interpreted to mean that those who had died would "come back to life" or "be resurrected" at the legendary "Final Judgement."

Esoterically, it has several meanings, the most important of which are:

1. That the many faculties and spiritual powers of man which are presently dormant or inactive will be "awakened" and activated by the quickening power of the Spirit.

2. That many of the things which we have done, said,

and experienced but forgotten, will be remembered and
brought to consciousness again when spiritual consciousness
will illuminate us.

3. That eventually, man will acquire spiritual consciousness, Life Eternal, or conscious immortality
and thus be "resurrected" from the "dead."

This "resurrection" will take place at different points
in different degrees in one's spiritual evolution. It
does take place, to a certain extent, when we pass on
to the "other side", and when we pray with great
fervor, or *consciously* receive the Sacraments.

Its fullest and highest form will take place at the time
of our spiritual Initiation.

"And the life of the ages to come."

Exoterically, this meant that man's consciousness does
not perish at death and still lives on.

Esoterically, it continues and completes the foregoing
statement, pointing to the fact that man will continue his
evolution and eventually attain conscious immortality, or
Life Eternal.

Chapter Nine

THE BEATITUDES:
THEIR NATURE AND USE

The Beatitudes is another very important document which constitutes a major pillar of the theoretical and practical training of the Western Spiritual Tradition.

As a whole, the Beatitudes contain a blueprint of man's conscious spiritual evolution and of how he may deliberately enter the Path of genuine self-actualization and Self-realization through graded steps.

As such, they can be used for concentration, meditation, and contemplation exercises, for theurgic work, and for establishing a vital link between the conscious and the super-conscious.

Text of the Prayer:
> "Blessed are the poor in spirit: for theirs is the Kingdom of Heaven.
> Blessed are they that mourn: for they shall be comforted.
> Blessed are the meek: for they shall inherit the Earth.
> Blessed are they which do hunger and thirst after righteousness: for they shall be filled.
> Blessed are the merciful: for they shall obtain mercy.

Blessed are the pure in heart: for they shall see God.
Blessed are the peacemakers: for they shall be called
the children of God.
Blessed are they which are persecuted for righteousness sake: for theirs is the Kingdom of Heaven.
Blessed are ye, when men shall revile you, and shall
say all manner of evil against you falsely, for My
sake. Rejoice and be exceedingly glad; for great is
your reward in Heaven."

"Blessed are the poor in spirit: for theirs is the Kingdom of Heaven."

This formula, sung or recited antiphonically, represents
the dialogue between the Higher Self and the lower self, and
in so doing, it blazes open a psychic channel between the
superconscious and the conscious.

1. To bless means to establish a consciousness and
   energy channel whereby higher energies and vibrations
   can flow into the lower ones and the lower energies
   can tune into higher ones.
2. To be poor in spirit means, here, to feel a lack, and
   therefore a desire for something that one feels is very
   important.
3. The Kingdom of Heaven is the higher state of
   consciousness in which spiritual consciousness is
   operating and where one would experience one's true
   Self, God's Wisdom and Love, and the goodness of
   Creation.

In light of the explanation of the above formula, this
means: those who feel a great lack and desire for spiritual
things will eventually be blessed by the Divine Spark as they
seek them.

A channel or "Ladder of Jacob" is then established
between the conscious and the superconscious. Through this
channel, higher energies and consciousness will flow into

one's human consciousness eventually flooding it with Light and awakening true spiritual consciousness.

By vibrating this petition theurgically, one should visualize one's Head Center, Kether, being awakened, and a dazzling white light formulating around this area.

"Blessed are they that mourn: for they shall be comforted."

"They that mourn" are those that are seeking what they feel is very important to them, which they feel they are lacking but which they desire intensely.

"They shall be comforted" means that eventually they will find that which they seek: they will be "blessed" by the Divine Spark and will attain spiritual consciousness which is the Kingdom of Heaven.

This second affirmation tells us that to achieve Illumination and spiritual consciousness, one must "mourn" for it, i.e. desire it intensely, involve one's emotions with it, which will bring down "blessings" from the Divine Spark and eventually, Illumination, which is the only thing that can bring true and lasting comfort to a human being. As such, this affirmation reinforces and continues the operation of the first.

Theurgically, the devotee would experience his left cheek center, Chokmah, being awakened.

"Blessed are the meek: for they shall inherit the Earth."

We have already discussed the esoteric meaning of the word "to bless," which is to transfer consciousness and life from a higher source to a lower one.

"The meek", esoterically speaking, are neither those who are passive, timid, or cowardly, nor those who will not fight for their self-respect and rights. Rather, in this context, the "meek" indicate those who are open, receptive to the Light, and to the flow of inspiration and intuition coming down from "above" and who will not "block it off" or resist it.

"The Earth" refers, on the one hand, to man's normal

state of consciousness, and, on the other hand, to man's physical body and to his "little Kingdom" or personality.

The whole formula therefore means, esoterically, that those who are open and receptive to the Light and the higher inspiration, who do not 'drown it out', or "struggle against" the Will of God, of the Divine Spark Within, will "inherit the Earth," i.e. achieve a psychosynthesis around the center of their higher Self and acquire self-mastery, which is one of the major objectives of all true spiritual training.

It also points to the fact there is a time in life to face whatever forces that confront us, and there is a time to bend to them so as to husband one's resources to be used again at a later time; for the tree that bends to the wind will not be broken while the tree that cannot bend might be uprooted.

Theurgically, this Beatitude activates the right cheek Center, Binah.

"Blessed are they which do hunger and thirst after righteousness: for they shall be filled."

This formula reminds us that those who seek will eventually find what they are seeking, irrespective of how long and hard the search might be; it also reminds us that we must desire righteousness, i.e. what is right, the Will of the Divine in us, as much as we can hunger and thirst for food and water, if we are to make true spiritual progress.

Finally, it tells us that to be filled with Divine Light, to flood our stream of awareness with spiritual energies, we must desire them and hunger for them with all our heart and soul.

The theurgic use of this ritual would be the activation of the left shoulder Center, Chesed.

"Blessed are the merciful: for they shall obtain "mercy."

This affirmation, whose central symbol is mercy, can be esoterically interpreted from two basic standpoints: that of the microcosm and that of the macrocosm.

From the standpoint of the macrocosm, it points to man's relationship with the world and shows that as man treats others, so they, in turn, will treat him; that if he shows mercy (tolerance, understanding, and compassion) towards others, so they in turn will show mercy towards him.

Underpinning this relationship stands the law of Cause and Effect, the law of Action and Reaction, or what is known esoterically as the law of Karma.

Looking at the petition from the standpoint of the microcosm, it points to the relationship of man's conscious with the superconscious.

Mercy is the title and key attribute of Chesed, and Chesed is the highest of man's "existential Sephiroth", or psychospiritual Centers which connects him with the Supernals.

Underpinning the relationship of man to the Supernals is the law of "like attracts like" and that in order to make "Gold" one must have "Gold". As man cultivates and expresses mercy in his daily life, so higher spiritual Energies will flow from the superconscious into his consciousness.

As man gives to his fellowman, so he will receive from the Divine Spark; as man treats his fellowman on the horizontal dimension, so will his inner psychic structure enable his Divine Spark to deal with him.

Theurgically, one awakens one's Right Shoulder Center, Geburah, with this affirmation.

"*Blessed are the pure in heart: for they shall see God.*"
The "pure in heart" has, understandably, several meanings and correspondences on several levels of consciousness. The major ones for our present purposes are:
1. To have a Heart Center that is cleansed, awakened, and balanced.
2. To have an Aura or Sphere of Sensation that has been cleansed, balanced, and spiritualized by the

Light of God.

   3.   To have noble, pure, elevating emotions, desires, and
        aspirations, i.e. to love and to yearn after the Divine
        Light, justice, goodness, and wholesomeness.

   To "see God" can also have several meanings, chief of
which are:

   1.   To become aware of, and experience, the Divine
        Presence, the Life of the Divine Spark.
   2.   To feel the Divine Light rushing into our Sphere of
        Sensation and quickening the whole field of human
        consciousness.
   3.   To see the Divine Light in ourselves and in others as
        our Divine Spark becomes conscious of Itself in our
        human Temple.

   This formula is designed to guide man to examine,
purify, and raise his motives, intentions, and aspirations so
that by purifying his emotions and intentions, he may enable
the Divine Light to flow into him, and to quicken him into a
new and higher state of consciousness.

   On the Theurgic level, this petition opens the Heart
Center, Tiphareth.

"Blessed are the peacemakers: for they shall be called the children of God."

   "Peacemakers" can again be interpreted horizontally,
in the world, and vertically, in man. Horizontally, a 'peacemaker' is one who helps to settle conflicts and disputes
between human beings, who brings about social peace or
social integration.

   Vertically, a "peacemaker is one who brings peace or
harmony in his own psyche (one who strives to achieve his
own psychosynthesis). It is also one who works to harmonize
his human faculties with the Divine Will and Life in him; by
that we mean one who strives for union with God or a
Spiritual Psychosynthesis.

The Beatitudes: Their Nature and Use / 145

As a whole, this formula points to the fact that those who strive for peace, for a personal, interpersonal and trans-personal psychosynthesis will be 'blessed', or in other words, they will receive an outpouring of Divine Light from the Divine Spark.

In this petition one activates one's Left Hip Center, Netzach, when doing theurgic work.

"Blessed are they which are persecuted for righteousness sake: for theirs is the Kingdom of Heaven."

To be "persecuted for righteousness sake" means to be willing to suffer, to undergo hardships and persecutions for the sake of doing what one knows to be right. Moreover, it requires a great deal of FAITH (concentration, understanding, and love) and of conviction in what one knows to be right.

Finally, it demands a great deal of effort of the will, which then further develops and strengthens the will.

Unless man has the courage and the strength to fight and to suffer for what he believes to be right, he is not ready for and will not be able to implement the promptings of his Divne Spark.

This faith, courage, conviction, and willpower must be developed on the Path before one can reach true Illlumination. However, once they are developed, and when one is willing and able to follow the dictates of one's higher conscience regardless of the personal implications these have for one's social and material well-being in the world, then one will find oneself well on the way to spiritual Illumination.

Two important "hints" to this formula are:

1. In order to "speed up" one's evolution and pay one's Karmic debts as one is treading the Path of spiritual growth, all kinds of afflictions, persecutions, and trials are likely to befall the candidate.

2. That society and social conscience being what they are, it is hardly possible to live in this world and obey

the dictates of one's higher conscience, rather than those of society, without being misunderstood and persecuted.

But, for those that are spiritually enlightened, even these persecutions and afflictions have their *raison d'etre* and perform a useful function in God's Plan.

If using this petition in a theurgic setting, one would activate the Right Hip Center, Hod.

"Blessed are ye, when men shall revile you, and shall say all manner of evil against you falsely for my sake. rejoice and be exceedingly glad; for great is your reward in Heaven."

As hinted in the previous explanation, when a candidate enters the spiritual Path and begins to tread it firmly, he leaves the large and winding road of evolution that most human beings travel on for the much narrower and steeper Path wherein he will meet fewer souls. In so doing, two basic things can be expected:

1. He will have trials, tests, hardships, and tribulations that will seem to fall upon him from all sides.

   He will compress in a few months and years the experiences and lessons he would normally have undergone over a much longer period of time.

   He will greatly accelerate the paying up of past Karma and will be tempted and tested much beyond what most men and women are.

   As an old saying rightfully puts it: "laugh and the world will laugh with you; cry, and you will cry alone."

2. His values and basic principles will change noticeably, first in his human consciousness and then in his overt behavior.

   Rather than living by the values and dictates of his society, he will do what the voice of his Higher Self prompts him to do regardless of personal and social consequences. Naturally, in doing so, he will incur the displeasure, the misunderstanding, and the persecutions of many.

If indeed it is the voice of his higher Self, his Divine Spark, and not the voice of his pride, of his reason, or of some other subconscious or sociocultural entity he is following and suffering for, two things will normally ensue:

1. He will greatly strengthen and further develop his FAITH, his determination, and his will-power, and thus unfold valuable psychospiritual faculties.
2. Once his tests and ordeals in the world are over, he will rapidly expand his consciousness, unfold spiritual consciousness, and obtain his "reward", or the fruits of the Great Work, in the higher states of consciousness (in Heaven).

It is well known that society fears and attacks the unfamiliar—those who do not conform to its standards and norms. Because of this, two opposite types of "deviants" are always persecuted and reviled as outcasts by society: those who are further ahead in evolution—the Saints and the spiritually enlightened human beings, and those who are behind in evolution—the criminals, the idiots, and the insane.

This document clearly outlines the work and prepares the candidate to enter into and walk upon the Path of Spiritual Initiation.

And finally, the theurgic practitioner activates Yesod, the Root or Sexual Center with the first part of this formula: "Blessed are ye, when men shall revile you and shall say all manner of evil against you falsely for my sake", and Malkuth, the Feet Center, with the second part: "Rejoice and be exceedingly glad; for great is your reward in Heaven"."

Chapter Ten

THE HAIL MARY:
ITS NATURE AND USE

In many of the old liturgies, and particularly in the liturgies of the Orthodox Church, the Hail Mary was formulated as follows:

Text of the Prayer:
> "The Mother of the Lord and Light-giver, let us exalt: Hail O Birth-giver Mary, full of grace, the Lord is with Thee.
> Blessed are Thou amongst women and blessed is the fruit of Thy womb.
> For Thou hast borne the Savior of our Souls."

This prayer, short and simple as it is, is one of the "Seven Fundamentals." Thus it is a most important spiritual document containing profound esoteric knowledge and a series of integrated and practical exercises designed to establish a breakthrough between the conscious and the superconscious, to fill the human Aura with spiritual Light, and to harmonize man's human self with his Spiritual Self.

Mother of the Lord and Light-giver;

This refers to man's *soul,* his Tree of Life and Aura, whence the Light flows and which must someday become the "Birth-giver" or matrix for the Christ-consciousness.

In the world, it is the *Anima Mundi,* the soul of the world, or the Earth's collective psychic atmosphere. In history, Mary, the mother of the Master Jesus, became the archetype, or perfect symbol and personification of the human soul and of the *Anima Mundi.* She was an advanced Initiate who became the Earthly Mother of the man in whom the *Christ Spirit* would incarnate fully and consciously.

Mary, therefore, represents the ideal woman, the perfection of the female principle, and the incarnation of the eternal feminine aspect—a part which we all have within our being!

To exalt the "Light-giver" is to focus all our attention upon the soul and the Tree of Life, so as to raise its vibratory rate and to heighten our state of consciousness, so that it will indeed become a Light and Life-giver, the seat of the Christ-consciousness for ourselves and for the world.

Hail O Birth-giver Mary, full of grace, the Lord is with Thee.

This exercise contains one of the most important and powerful spiritual exercises that man can use to fill his soul with Light, to raise his vibratory level, and to expand his consciousness. As with all other spiritual exercises, it demands FAITH to make it operational— a great deal of concentration, visualization, and some understanding of what one is doing and why, and finally, a profound love for God and for the Great Work.

By saying "Hail O Birth-giver Mary," the devotee focuses all his attention and consciousness upon his soul, reminding himself (and then experiencing it, if possible) that his soul is the "Birth-giver", or matrix, for human consciousness on all planes and levels, and that it is in his Tree of Life within him, that God, Man, and Nature are "born," or spring forth into consciousness.

By adding "full of grace," the candidate now visualizes and experiences the Divine Light slowly *filling his entire Aura,* activating his entire Tree of Life, and spreading through all his levels of consciousness.

When performed with the utmost FAITH, and when the devotee is ready for it, this becomes one of the key exercises that will bring about the "Golden Dawn" of spiritual consciousness, which is the slow awakening of a higher and qualitatively different state of consciousness in man.

By concluding "the Lord is with Thee," the candidate affirms and should experience, if possible, the Divine Spark operating through him, and that the Spiritual Self is now manifesting Its energies through him. (This can only be possible to the extent that the soul, Tree of Life, and Aura have been purified and vitalized by the Divine Light.)

In a nutshell, this operation contains and represents the Great Work in its essence and the ultimate realization that all human beings must eventually come to: the union of God with man, and of the spiritual Self with the psyche so that human consciousness can now manifest and reflect the Spirit in the world.

By stating this fact and "prophecy," one does not realize it immediately but one builds a thoughtform and establishes the groundwork (the attitude and state of consciousness) which will eventually lead to its full realization.

On one level we have a *symbolic* representation of something (like a map of a country or a film showing some of its landscape) and on another level we have the realization of the petition (like being in the country and seeing the landscape with one's own eyes).

However, ideas and thoughtforms have a peculiar property: they are a *self-fulfilling prophecy* that contains an inner energy which drives man, both subconsciously and superconsciously, to realize and objectify them in the world.

Blessed art Thou amongst women and blessed is the fruit of Thy womb.

> Exoterically, this formula that was so often used by the Christian Church, meant that Mary was more blessed and pure than any other woman and that the fruit of her womb, Jesus, was also especially blessed in that He was the Son of God rather than the son of man. But this would make Mary a "special darling of God" which would represent an injustice and an arbitrariness on the part of God. This of course, is not, and cannot be so.
>
> Its true meaning, however, as with so many prayers, rituals, and spiritual documents, can only be discovered at the esoteric level when we interpret these symbols and analogies in terms of their correspondences in the microcosm.
>
> "Blessed amongst women" means two things, or one thing on two different levels:
>
> 1. That the woman, or human being, who succeeds in establishing a breakthrough or conscious contact with the Divine Spark will, indeed, be "blessed" amongst women or other human beings. 'Blessed" here means experiencing a transfer of life, energy and consciousness from a higher source to a

lower one.

2. That the feminine principle which succeeds in establishing a contact and rapport with the Divine Spark will, likewise, be "blessed" and enlivened.

"Blessed is the fruit of Thy womb" means that the 'being', or principle, to which the woman is giving birth is also "blessed."

Every woman and every feminine principle, which "woman" embodies, must give birth to some "being" or principle. For example, Love, if it is genuine, must and will bear fruit, but this "fruit" can appear on different planes of being. It can be a child on the physical plane, but it also can be a feeling, an idea, an intuition, a new insight, realization, or state of consciousness.

A female principle without love will remain barren and a barren female principle always remains an unfulfilled female principle.

Whatever is born always reflects the nature and origin of the male and female principles which gave birth to it, the "force" and the "form" which engendered it.

In this case, what is born, the "fruit", is *spiritual consciousness,* which is created by the marriage of the spiritual Self and the psyche which thus enters in contact with the Divine Spark which then blesses Its offspring in human consciousness.

For Thou hast borne the Savior of our souls.

Exoterically, the Savior of our souls is Jesus Christ; Esoterically, it is Divine Spark which engenders true spiritual consciousness in the Tree of Life and the human Aura.

Thus this last and completing formula concludes the

whole operation. At this point, the candidate should feel and experience that his soul is filled with the Divine Light and Life, and that spiritual consciousness is in direct contact with the spiritual Self, and that It alone is the Savior, i.e. the unifying and life-giving principle of his being and consciousness.

Let us look at this spiritual document from the perspective and vocabulary of psychosynthesis, which is the latest and most advanced of approaches of the modern human and social sciences.

a. "Hail O Birth-giver Mary, full of grace, the Lord is with thee."
This ascription can be interpreted here, as the student turns all his attention and consciousness towards his psyche and its functions, as: seeing them and sensing them being filled with the life and energies of the spiritual Self which harmonizes and integrates them into a true personal psychosynthesis. At a later and more advanced level, it means to actually experience and live this personal psychosynthesis.

b. "Blessed art Thou amongst women and blessed is the fruit of Thy womb."
This can be interpreted as the inrushing stream of intuition and inspiration flowing from the spiritual Self and the superconscious into the field of consciousness, the human self, and the seven functions of the psyche, as an unbroken and two-way stream. The devotee must first *visualize* and then *feel* and *experience* this process taking place within himself.

c. "For Thou hast borne the Savior of our souls."
This final petition would be understood to mean the recognition that the final unfoldment, coordination, and integration of all of man's faculties can only

come about through a spiritual psychosynthesis.
At a later and more advanced stage, the student must have an actual personal experience of that spiritual psychosynthesis whereby the spiritual Self can now flow into and become the "human self" of man and express Its attributes through the seven functions of man's psyche in his life and in the world.

Here we can see that the perspective and terminology are different but the fundamental principles and truths remain the same for anyone (or any system) who has truly decoded and penetrated into its central core and who has had a direct personal experience of it.

Chapter Eleven

THE TEN COMMANDMENTS: THEIR NATURE AND USE

To understand the deeper nature, the philosophical and ethical implications, and practical applications of the Ten Commandments, we must first turn to their exoteric and historical meaning—for the path to the esoteric depths and mysteries always begins with the outer, the exoteric, or the "letter" of the teachings.

This is, generally, the reason why before one can begin to ascend towards the heights of the Spirit and the descent towards the depths of the unconscious, one must have *memorized* and *mastered* the outer or "letter" of spiritual teachings.

Both the world religions and the true Mystery Schools acknowledge this principle and require it of their devotees and students.

Let us therefore begin by briefly looking at the historical and traditional circumstances through which the Ten Commandments were given to humanity for many deeper or esoteric secrets concerning their nature and application are contained there for those who have "eyes to see" and "ears to hear".

Then we shall proceed to look at their orthodox or

157

"literal" interpretation and at the major sociocultural impact they had, as an ethical system, upon Western civilization.

Finally, after this necessary preamble, we shall turn to an in-depth and detailed study of their esoteric or spiritual meanings and applications.

Again, let the serious and mature student bear in mind that the true "esoteric" and "spiritual secrets" cannot be found in some "occult school" or "esoteric doctrine", but, rather, in the well-known though generally little understood teachings and symbols of the great world religions, and throughout the world of *nature* which we can behold every day; more importantly, these "arcane principles and mysteries" are not so much to be grasped and discussed intellectually as they are to be *lived* and *experienced* in the depths and heights of one's being *in one's daily life.*

This is why "serious and mature students" are one thing and "curiosity seekers" another, and why genuine schools and orders are continually seeking to discriminate between the former and the latter.

In the Bible, we can find the following account of how the Ten Commandments were given to mankind:

> In the third month after the departure of the children of Israel out of the land of Egypt . . . they came to the wilderness of Sinai and the encampment in the wilderness; and there Israel camped before the mountain.
>
> And Moses went up to God and God called him out of the mountain and said to him . . . "If you will obey my voice indeed and keep my covenant, then shall you be my beloved ones above all peoples, for all the Earth is mine . . .
>
> And the Lord said to Moses, "Lo, I am coming to you in a thick cloud, that the people may hear when I speak with you and also believe you forever . . .
>
> And it came to pass on the third day in the morning that there were thunders and lightnings, and a thick cloud appeared on the mountain . . .
>
> And the whole mountain of Sinai was smoking because the Lord descended upon it in fire; and the smoke thereof ascended like the smoke of a furnace, and the whole mountain quaked greatly.

And when the blast of the trumpet sounded long and grew louder and louder, Moses spoke and God answered him by voice.

And the Lord came down upon mount Sinai; to the very top of the mountain;

and Moses went up . . .

And God spoke all these words saying: "I am the Lord your God, who brought you out of the land of Egypt, out of the house of bondage. You shall have no other Gods except me.

You shall not make for yourself any graven image, or any likeness of anything that is in the Earth beneath or that is in the water under the Earth . . .

You shall not take a false oath in the name of the Lord your God; for the Lord will not declare him innocent who takes an oath in his name falsely.

Remember the Sabbath day to keep it holy. Six days shall you labor and do your work; but the seventh day is a sabbath to the Lord your God; in it you shall not do any work . . . For in six days the Lord made Heaven and Earth, the seas, and all things that are in them, and rested on the seventh day . . .

Honor your father and your mother, that your days may be long upon the land which the Lord your God gives you.

You shall not kill.

You shall not commit adultery.

You shall not covet your neighbor's house. You shall not covet your neighbor's wife . . . nor anything that is your neighbor's . . . "

And all the people observed the thundering and the lightning flashes and the sound of the trumpet and the mountain smoking and when the people saw this, they were afraid and stood far off.

And the Lord said to Moses . . . "an altar of earth shall you make to me, and you shall sacrifice on it your burnt offerings and your peace offerings, your sheep and your oxen; in every place where I shall make a memorial to my name I will come to you and I will bless you."

(Exodus 20: 1-24)

The Ten Commandments, as given by Moses to the Israelites at the foot of Mount Sinai, have generally been interpreted at a literal level according to the historical and cultural definitions assigned them by a given religion and by a given people who adopted them.

These Ten Commandments, in their various definitions

and forms of interpretation have provided the ethical corner-stone and the central core of all theoretical and practical ethical systems of the various Western civilizations. The very life and survival of a group, or nation, has largely depended upon them.

Moreover, their functional equivalents, with slight differences of wording and interpretation, can also be found in other religions and in the Eastern cults, whether in the Buddhist, Shintoist, Confucian, or Hindu systems.

Therefore these commandments in their exoteric interpretation can be seen as constituting the core elements necessary to enable a human society to function as a viable system and to endure through time.

Two central points can be made in terms of their *exoteric* interpretation:

1. That the Ten Commandments have essentially one basic meaning and interpretation which are defined by the religious and social authorities of a given society and which are valid for all members of that society.

2. That this one basic meaning and interpretation, given by the Church and the state, deals essentially with man's attitudes and behavior patterns in the world towards his church, his state, and his fellowmen.

Just as we found two basic points characterizing the exoteric interpretation of the Ten Commandments so, now, we can establish three main points that characterize their esoteric interpretation.

1. The Ten Commandments are seen as an open symbolic system with many different meanings, interpretations, correspondences, and applications which change and expand with our degree of maturity and experience in life and, particularly, with our state of consciousness. To different states of consciousness correspond different meanings, associations, and applications of the Ten Commandments.

2. The esoteric interpretation of the Ten Commandments focuses essentially upon an explanation and application of the Ten Commandments *within* man's "little kingdom."

3. The esoteric or spiritual approach looks at the Ten Commandments not only as a set of ethical and philosophical guidelines to regulate human interaction but also as a set of practical spiritual exercises designed to bring about the completion and perfection of man.

From the esoteric standpoint, the conditions under which the Ten Commandments were given to mankind are highly significant and indicative of their origin, nature, and application.

The Ten Commandments were given to Moses on top of Mount Sinai after a long period of wandering in the wilderness in quest of the promised land. It was God, the Lord, or Divine Spark, who revealed them to Moses, the leader and most evolved Initiate of his nation, amidst "light", "fire,", and "smoke".

Moses represents the prototype, the living exemplar of the true Initiate of all times. Hence, it is not so much that we have to look up to Moses or follow his teachings as it is that we must *become what he was.*

Moses is also the symbol of the higher human consciousness a man can develop by his own efforts. Thus, esoterically speaking, this event refers to an inner experience that every human being can have.

At this point, man's higher consciousness (obtained through his efforts and experiences) must climb on the sacred Mountain of Consciousness towards the top where the superconscious resides with the Divine Spark. There the Lord (the spiritual consciousness of the Divine Spark) will descend towards it with a manifestation of Light and Fire and will reveal the Divine Laws ruling all creation.*

---

*creation: the Tree of Life on the Four Worlds: Aziluth, Divine consciousness; Briah, the superconscious; Yetzirah, the conscious; and Assiah, the unconscious.

The fog and smoke seen drawing a 'curtain' between the top of the mountain where Moses climbs and the base of the mountain where the people reside symbolize the veil or curtain that separates the superconscious from the normal consciousness.

All human beings at a certain point in their spiritual development can and will have the experience that Moses had on Mount Sinai. For the living laws of God and creation are buried deep within the higher reaches of human conscious, and the Divine Spark in each of us will reveal them "in spirit and in truth" when we truly seek them and have prepared ourselves to receive them worthily (when we are *ready* and *capable* of putting them into practice and of "living them").

Moreover, as we expand and raise our consciousness and as we mature through experience on Earth, we shall discover ever greater and deeper meanings, correspondences, and applications of these laws of which the Ten Commandments are the blueprint and the symbolic representation. The deeper meanings of the Ten Commandments will be revealed to us by the Divine Spark, (through the power of the Holy Spirit as the Bible says) as we seek to live and to incarnate them in our being.

To quote an advanced student of the Mysteries:

The Ten Commandments contain very specific theoretical and practical information and exercises for the unfoldment of our psyche and of our spiritual powers—which alone can, ultimately, satisfy the hunger of our souls . . .

The way to spiritual attainment goes through a very long, steep, and dangerous path wherein Divine Guidance is absolutely necessary. The central goal of all spiritual development is and can only be *union with God*. The attainment of all psychic and spiritual powers are actually secondary to this great goal, a by-product of it, as it were. One of the major means by which to achieve this great goal is to live by God's Laws, to incorporate the teachings of all world saviors in our mental and psychic being, to live them and exemplify them— there is simply no substitute for this.

Prayer, and its living application in daily life, is also invaluable to enable us to establish a direct personal contact with the higher Planes of Consciousness and Being. The guidance and protection of God's Servants is also of inestimable value for man's proper human and spiritual development.

For man today in his ignorance, arrogance, and metaphysical thirst, is constantly creating new speculations, metaphysical cults, and methods of self-realization which neglect or assign secondary importance to the fundamental teachings of all world religions (which are the legitimate channels for the slow but safe improvement and spiritualization of mankind). Few of the blind leaders of the blind have even bothered to read, to comprehend, and to live the teachings of the world religions. The seven Sacraments, correlated with the seven lower Sephiroth, and the seven Initiations lead man gradually and by degrees from animality to spirituality, to true Adepthood— without getting one lost and confused in the jungles of homespun speculation and philosophizing.

True Christianity, both exoteric and esoteric, finds its fulfillment in the Ten Commandments amplified and completed by the Two Commandments of Christ (Love the Lord thy God with all thy heart, all thy soul, and all thy mind; and thy fellow-men as thyself). This forms the true basis of training for genuine Illumination and Adepthood.

You must keep in mind, however, that only preliminary training is given on the physical plane; the real and advanced training is given on the Inner Planes. True spiritual consciousness transcends both the five senses and psychism. A balanced and healthy character and life must be achieved before real training can begin.

Our civilization and all of our penal codes ultimately stand upon the Ten Commandments—which are so much neglected in the current 'psychic' and 'occult' literature and which are generally despised by modern man. Only when man has learned to live by the Ten Commandments—something which is known to the Higher Powers—can man begin his real spiritual training.

Man's spiritual consciousness and development depend upon the activation of his ten Spiritual Centers or Organs which are perfectly matched with the Ten Commandments. The activation of these 'Organs' depend strictly upon their being used and awakened by appropriate exercises and by life itself. The Ten Commandments in their practical applications are a very effective and time-proven set of exercises specifically designed to awaken our spiritual Centers. As the 22nd Chapter of Revelation puts it: 'Blessed are they that do His Commandments, that they may have the right to the Tree of Life, and may enter through the Gates of the City.' And 'to him that overcometh (the lower self), and he will become a Pillar in my Temple and shall go out (incarnate on earth) no more.'

The Ten Commandments, being among other things practical exercises to awaken and activate the ten spiritual Centers, must be placed on the Tree of Life and *vibrated** (i.e. affirmed) each in its appropriate sphere; then they must be meditated upon to discover their deeper meanings and correspondences, and finally, they must be lived and incorporated in our being.

Each one of the spiritual Centers is a 'living entity,' and 'executive' in its respective department.

The first Commandment rules all the others. It is the Divine Spark in man addressing his human self and the human personality. It affirms its rulership and projects Light into all the other Centers. Each of these Centers, symbolized by the sign of a Planet thus becomes activated in the constellation . . . which is man! Thus it is that we have ten Centers to awaken and activate by the Ten Commandments, to transmute our vices into virtues, our imperfections and imbalances into perfection and harmony.

Keep in mind the admonition: "If thou wilt enter into the consciousness of Life Eternal, keep the Commandments, practice them, live them, realize them in thyself, become them."

Now stand up erect and relaxed, face East and begin with the affirmation: 'Be silent and know that I am the Lord thy God' or 'Know ye not that ye are the Temple of the living God and that the Spirit of God dwells in you.' (After having gone through the preliminary preparation of breathing, cleansing, and spiritual awakening through the Cross Ritual.) †

Let us now look at the Ten Commandments, taken one by one, in terms of their esoteric or spiritual interpretation. The following is offered by way of example of what can be done with them and is not the only set of esoteric meanings, correspondences, and applications that can be given to them; for these are many, ever changing and deepening with the

---

*In the Spiritual Traditions, to "vibrate" a God-Name or a Name of Power implies either to chant this Word physically or to utter this Name of Power silently within one's consciousness, PUTTING ONE'S WHOLE MIND, HEART, AND SOUL INTO THEM, i.e. concentrating one's whole attention upon it, directing all of one's thoughts to it, and pouring one's emotions and love into it.

† *SRIA Documents*

expansion of human consciousness. They do represent some of the most basic and fundamental ones that can be used both theoretically, for knowledge-getting, and practically, for spiritual growth.

I am the Lord thy God, thou shall have no other gods before me.

I am: refers to man's Divine Spark or Spiritual Self.

Thou shall have no other gods before me: implies that no other principle or entity in man's being other than the Divine Spark should become his Center, the integrating and unifying principle of his psyche and life.

In man's being and life, there are presently many principles and entities which become, temporarily at least, his "God" or synthesizing Center. These "gods" or partial synthesizing foci can be: his body and its instincts and sensations, his emotions and strong passions, his mind and powerful thoughts or *'idee fixes,'* or even his mystical experiences; the major social roles he plays in society and with which he generally identifies; and finally, the living or historical "model" of another human being.

By vibrating and affirming this Commandment in Kether, one temporarily identifies with the spiritual Self, the Divine Spark within and affirms Its rulership in his being and life in all of their dimensions and aspects. It affirms in other words: "Let the Divine Spark in me be my true self and rule my being."

This Commandment thus sums up the whole program of spiritual development; it shows man what he must accomplish while here on Earth and helps him to do so temporarily and to slowly and gradually bring about this condition on a permanent basis; union with the Spiritual Self and Its rulership in our "little kingdom" and in our daily life.

Thou shall not make idols of me nor bow down to worship and serve them.

The key symbol of this Commandment is the word

"idols" which comes from the Greek "eidolon", meaning images or thoughtforms.

This Commandment continues the process set in motion by the first. It is not enough to affirm that it is the Spiritual Self rather than the many "human selves" (subpersonalities) of man that he should identify with and establish as the Center or unifying principle of his being and life. There is a basic difference between the spiritual Self, Its Life and Consciousness, and the many possible mental representations and symbols that man can create about the Spiritual Self during his long evolutionary journey.

This Commandment thus stresses the basic difference between "form" and "force", between a mental representation and a living reality, between a concept and an experience.

Consciousness, in order to formulate and to express itself, needs the twin polarities of form and force, and man must use symbols and representations of Higher Beings, Realities, and States of Consciousness, but he must be aware of what they are: a means to an end, and not the reality which they represent.

For man, the ultimate form or vehicle (called the "temple" by the various religious traditions) is the psyche, the human aura and the Tree of Life, and not a mental representation.

Man has created countless "idols" or "images" of the Spiritual Self which he has represented on icons, statues, or words, and he has worshipped many gods (money, sex, and power being amongst the more popular ones).

This Commandment is also designed to help man differentiate between the Divine Spark Itself and Its Life and Consciousness that reside in the upper reaches of human consciousness, and the many mental representations of It which are lifeless, that man has made of It.

This is the affirmation which enables man to distinguish between the Creator and Creation, between force and form, and to unite and integrate the two within his consciousness.

Vibrated in Chokmah, this affirmation enables man to acquire a true perspective of himself, of his fellow-men, and of God, which is true Wisdom.

Thou shall not use the Name of the Lord thy god in vain.

> *Use the Name of God in vain:* Exoterically, to use lightly or irreverently *any* Name of God or Name of Power. Esoterically, however, it means much more . . . The Name of God implies His Presence, His Consciousness, His Life and Energies.

This affirmation, vibrated in Binah, means not to abuse one's being, which is the "Temple" of the Divine Spark, in any way—not to misuse or drain one's energies, and the Light and Life one receives from "on high", or one's consciousness, emotions, thoughts, and desires in such a way as to cut them off from their central Source which is the One Reality, or the Spiritual Self.

Man presently abuses himself and his energies in countless ways on the physical, emotional, and mental levels. By not "using the Name of God in vain", man achieves and maintains harmony with his Divine Spark and becomes harmless to other beings . . . and to himself.

Thou shall keep holy the day of the Lord thy God.

> *To keep Holy:* means to preserve the harmony, the relationship or connectedness that will keep something whole or balanced.

> *The day of the Lord:* has several meanings and correspondences, chief of which are: the amount of time dedicated to God, or to direct spiritual work (establishing contact with the Divine-within on the vertical axis through Prayer). It also implies the spiritual plane and spiritual consciousness through which the Divine can be contacted, and the seven-fold cycle of

activity in which each phase has its own distinctive characteristics.

The Lord thy God: clearly refers to the Divine Spark at the core of one's being.

One of the most important tasks that man can accomplish while here on Earth is to create, to forge and fashion his own "little world"—to bring about a *psychosocial* cosmos out of chaos. Furthermore, the creation of man's own universe involves structuring his space, time, and actions. Therefore, this Commandment can be seen as dealing with the proper structuring of man's time so as to make it *flow whole,* and to live a *whole*some life.

The major periods of time for man are: the day, the week, the month, and the year. This Commandment calls man's attention to the fact that during each period of time, a day, a week, a month, a year, even a lifetime, he should periodically set some time aside for turning his focused attention to the Divine within, to actively seek to align his consciousness and life with the Will of the Divine Spark and to raise his consciousness on the "Holy Mountain" to the point where he can come in conscious contact with the Living Light and Fire, Love and Consciousness of the Divine-within.

This means keeping a proper balance and rhythm between Work, Prayer, and Relaxation, between his physical, human, and spiritual activities, and between his professional, personal, and spiritual life, and to tune into the various parts of his being and of the world which are material, psychic, and spiritual in nature.

In short, this affirmation deals with the mystery of life and growth, of rhythm and of proper structuring of time, and it focuses man's attention and energies upon Chesed which is the highest of the psychospiritual Centers which man can activate while being incarnate on Earth, and which represents Chronos or Time, called by the Greeks the "Father of the Gods."

Thou shall honor thy Father and thy Mother.

Thou: refers to the human self, the conscious rational ego acting within the field of consciousness.

Honor: to become aware of, to focus one's attention upon;

to enter into a proper relationship with;

to give and receive what is "due."

Father: the Spirit which is both within man and in the world: God and the Divine Spark which are one in essence;

the male principle which operates both in man's being and in his life, in what he is and what he does.

Mother: Nature, the physical plane which is both in man (his body) and in the world;

the female principle, which operates both in man's being and in his life, in what he is and in what he does.

"To honor one's Father and one's Mother" thus means:

a. To become aware that one is both Spirit and Matter and that so is the world. To enter into a proper relationship with the body, the Divine Spark within, and with God and Nature in the world. To give and to receive, to abide by the laws of the Spirit and of Nature—to give God what is His due and the world what is its due, i.e. to realize that one has both spiritual and physical needs.

b. To become aware that one is both male and female, and that there are times when one should act in a dynamic way, affirming one's self and one's ideas, and times when one should act in a passive way, receiving and accepting what comes to one.

c. It means to become aware of and to synthesize properly the myriad of masculine and feminine forces, energies, and polarities which constitute and mould our being, existence, and becoming: the subjective/objective, prayer/work, knowledge/love, severity/mercy, grace/effort, asceticism/joie de vivre, joy/pain, spirit/matter, good/evil, accepting one's fate and struggling against it.

This Commandment focuses upon Geburah and awakens it by connecting it with Chesed, synthesizing their energies and principles. It is the commandment dealing with the mystery of polarity and the realization of synthesis on many levels.

Thou shall not kill.

This Commandment implies not to destroy that which exists before its "natural time" for disintegration has come, be it a human being, a creature, an intuition, thought, feeling, or deed.

It is the principle which deals with reverence for life both generically and specifically. It means, essentially, not to create disharmonies and not to interfere with what exists, both within and without one's self by the imposition of one's will and ideas, but to fulfill one's role, mission, and place in life according to God's Will and thus to consciously harmonize one's self with the Divine Spark and Its Plan of Evolution.

This Commandment also deals with unfolding the feminine, receptive, and harmonizing principle within one's self and in one's life. It is linked with Tiphareth and activates its energies and principles, synthesizing within itself all that descends from above and all that which ascends from below. For example, to suffocate someone with affection is just as much a violation of this Commandment as it would be starving someone's emotional needs with too much austerity.

It is at this level that the true synthesis of Chesed and Geburah, mercy and severity, is realized within one's being and life.

Thou shall not commit adultery.

The key symbol here is adultery, and from the esoteric

standpoint, adultery means to lose the state of pureness and clearness, concentration and integration that one can possess.

It also implies to split or dissociate the psyche from some of its functions, components and energies. This can take place by desiring or willing the wrong thing or the right thing at the wrong time.

It means that one should not unite, mate, or establish a "circuit" (take into one's aura or link one's aura) with the being, energy, or entity which is not for you, which is not on your path of evolution.

Properly understood and lived by it leads one to unite and mate on all levels, only according to God's Will as this is made manifest in one's being and life. For example, to do something only because it is "practical," "expedient," or easier are all instances of "commiting adultery."

This Commandment focuses on Netzach, activates it, cleanses it, or pollutes it when it is violated. It deals with the mystery of desire, wanting, and willing on the conscious level. To want what is "wrong" for oneself brings dissociation, confusion and misery in its wake, whereas to want what is "right" for oneself brings synthesis, peace, clarity, certainty, and joy as its natural consequences.

Thou shall not steal.

This Commandment tells us plainly that we should not take what does not belong to us, whether a physical, emotional, mental, or spiritual thing; whether a person, an energy, or an object, and appropriate it to oneself.

It implies to know and to take only that which God sends to us for our own good and growth, and not to use our will and resources to get arbitrarily what we want at the moment.

It means to grow consciously and concretely in harmony with the Will of the Divine Spark ... and with our self, society, and nature, without either *forcing* or *hindering* this growth.

This Commandment focuses on Hod and activates it, and it also balances and connects Hod and its energies with Netzach and its energies.

Basically, it means how not to want and to do what is not for you, but to align your conscious ego with the Will and Energies of the Spiritual Self so as to bring about a true harmony and growth in your being and in your life.

Thou shall not bear false witness.

To "bear false witness" means either to affirm that which does not correspond to reality or to project a thought-form that is not anchored in life, a process which creates a dissociation within the psyche and which will, eventually, be revealed for what it is.

It also implies not thinking, feeling, saying, or acting on things which one knows are false.

Finally, it urges that one does not distort the image of things by adding or cutting, magnifying or diminishing, the reality of things.

In essence it means not to create any thoughtforms which are contrary to the Will of the Divine Spark, not to congest and confuse one's mind, emotions, and social relations with wishful thinking or fanciful emotions.

It enables man to preserve a healthy equilibrium between ideals and reality, between theory and practice, and between individual freedom and social constraint.

This Commandment focuses on Yesod; activates it, cleanses it, and brings it in proper alignment with the higher Centers and with Malkuth.

Thou shall not covet the wife or any of the possessions of thy neighbor.

This is the only Commandment which applies fully and literally to the material plane, as it deals with Malkuth by activating, cleansing and equilibrating it. It also complements the seventh Commandment on the physical plane (as the latter deals with the psychological plane and the motivational dimension).

In essence, it means: you will not desire to receive, be, or become anything but what you are, what you have, and what you can become according to the Will and Plan of the Divine Spark. It means that if you see something someone else has, that you should not desire to have it, or desire to 'be' it without working for it and creating it by your own efforts, once you have obtained the confirmation from the "voice within" that you are doing the right thing. If you violate this Commandment, what you would get would not be "yours," organic to your being, but external to you, and a *burden* for your human and spiritual unfoldment. Also it would most likely generate social conflict and bring about a struggle with others who want to "preserve what they have."

Finally, it also means not to want to evolve too quickly or too slowly, but to wait for the right moment and the natural unfolding of your faculties, energies, and experiences. To give, desire, or accept "gifts" indiscriminately is violating this Commandment. The "wife of thy neighbor" is not only his woman, but also his faculties and his female principle. The "possessions of thy neighbor" are not only what he has and owns but also what he is and has achieved.

All of these Commandments, laws and principles, prepare man by degrees to achieve the "incarnation of the Word" or the proper alignment of his human self from within the center of the field of consciousness with his Spiritual Self in the superconscious; and to receive an inflow of Light and Life that can permeate his whole being and touch every Center and Plane. Thus the whole Tree of Life is touched and affected, and every principle in man is nourished and aligned with the Divine Spark.

Man can mature and grow only through action and through the use of all his faculties and energies; the Ten

Commandments are the laws and principles which govern the ''right'' or harmonious use of all of man's faculties and energies and which make right human relations possible. The "Great Chain of Being" and the inner link and harmony are thus preserved from the Divine to the physical plane.

These Commandments also have an inner threefold subdivision:

a. The first Commandment deals with the Spirit or Spiritual Self and its conscious realization.

b. The second, third, and fourth Commandments deal with the manifestation of the Spiritual Light, Fire, and Life in Creation; with preserving the proper alignment, harmony, and flow between the Divine Spark and the various planes of creation, both within and outside of man.

c. The fifth to the tenth Commandments deal with the sphere of right human relationships and with the preservation of the proper harmony in one's interpersonal relationships so that the Light and the Life of the Divine Spark can flow through one's Tree of Life to others and from others to oneself in an unbroken and undistorted fashion.

Let us now look at the Ten Commandments from the standpoint of psychosynthesis. We can readily see that they contain all the key theoretical steps and practical exercises necessary to achieve a complete psychosynthesis and to consciously complete the creation of one's personality and being.

1. *I am the Lord thy God, thou shall have no other gods before me.*

This affirmation clearly deals with *Self-identification;* with asserting that the Divine Spark is the true Self and not the human self, or the psyche, or the functions of the psyche, or any of the social roles that one plays in society.

2. *Thou shall not make idols of me . . .*

   This affirmation points to the principle of disident-ification, warning against the pitfall of making any of the elements of the psyche or of the world the unifying Center of one's being and life.

3. *Thou shall not use the Name of the Lord thy God in vain.*

   This injunction deals with the proper use and transformations of spiritual and psychological energies, or with the principle of Alchemy, as it used to be called, or the principle of psychodynamics as it is now called by modern science.

4. *Thou shall keep holy the day of the Lord thy God.*

   This petition deals with the principle of timing, rhythm, and cycles. Its aim is to sensitize one to the proper timing and balance in one's growth and daily acitivies.

5. *Thou shall honor thy Father and thy Mother.*

   This formula deals with the principle of polarity and gender, of properly relating spirit and matter, male and female, active and passive, which is so important in human life.

6. *Thou shall not kill.*

   This injunction deals with the principle of harmony, harmlessness, and proper alignment which is the goal of all true human and spiritual development.

7. *Thou shall not commit adultery.*

   This Commandment deals with the principle of purity and concentration which is vital to achieve anything worthwhile in this world.

8. *Thou shall not steal.*

   This Commandment deals with the principle of honesty and of respect for others.

9. *Thou shall not bear false witness.*

   This petition deals with the principle of honesty

and of objectivity.

10. *Thou shall not covet the wife or any of the possessions of thy neighbor.*

This injunction deals with the principle of right human relationships and with the principle of personal integrity which are necessary to live in harmony with others in social groups.

Each of the Commandments contains a positive and a negative aspect; an aspect of Light and an aspect of darkness, which activate, purify or sully the Centers on the Tree, the Planes of being, and the Self with the rest of the personality and with other human beings.

The Two Royal Commandments of the New Testament

If the Ten Commandents were the cornerstone of the Old Testament, the two Commandments given by Jesus are the cornerstone of the New Testament and are, in fact, the synthesis of all the Commandments—the very foundation of any type of genuine spiritual work.

These two commandments are:

"Thou shall love the Lord thy God with all thy heart, all thy soul, and all thy mind;

and thy fellow-men as thyself."

Though countless explanations, on different levels of consciousness and being could be given of these two Commandments, we shall limit ourselves to the most basic implications and applications.

These two commandments depict *symbolically* the interrelationship between the *Trinity* (Father, Son, and Holy Spirit; Wisdom, Love, and Will; God, Nature, and Man; the spiritual, the psychic, and the physical planes) and Duality (God and Man; Spirit and Matter; Male and Female). As such, they show man how he can consciously cooperate in his "becoming", in the fashioning and forging of his being, and in the realization of his perfection. Thus they deal with expanding meanings, correspondences, and applications on the mysteries of the Trinity and of Dualiy with their ever-the different planes of consciousness and being.

Man, who is an objectified and manifested emanation of the Trinity, (who is a triune being: spiritual, psychic, and physical) and who is the "microcosm" of the "macrocosm", operates both in the outer, or objective world (the horizontal axis on the 'Cross') and in the inner or subjective world (the vertical axis on the 'Cross'), and is thus a dual being.

Man must grow and expand both inwardly and outwardly on these two axes.

What flows into him from the higher reaches of his psyche must manifest itself outwardly in the world. This is the philosophical key to both genuine human development and to true spiritual life, as it is the foundation of the Great Work. (It is also the cognitive 'handle' by which to make *faith* and any ritual come alive and effective.)

Let us look at this last petition in terms of the mysteries of Duality, and then in terms of the mysteries of the Trinity which are also contained symbolically therein.

Love, Mystics have unanimously claimed, is both the first and the greatest force in the universe, as it is the manifestation of God's Will. The two most basic expressions of love which embodies the deepest needs and drives of man are the *love of God* and the *love of man* (the third being the love of nature which is God in manifestation here on Earth). Unless man learns consciously how to love both God and Man, he will never achieve any truly great thing as he will be cut off from the very roots of life. And it can safely be said that one of the greatest dilemmas of mankind is that of reconciling and integrating properly the love of God (spiritual love) and the love for mankind (human and physical love).

The whole life and growth of man really revolves around the movement of drawing the Light and Fire from the heights of his being, to express them in a concrete and constructive fashion through his words and deeds in the world. The progressive expansion of human consciousness, which is the Great Work of man, involves drawing ever higher "psychic voltage" or "life" from above, to which he must give definite sociocultural forms and expressions in the world.

The whole of spiritual life revolves around the twin concepts of worship (which represents the expression of the love of God) and of service (which represents the expression of the love of man). Putting these together we have the Cross; on the vertical axis thrusting towards God and on the horizontal axis thrusting towards man, which graphically forms the cornerstone of the true spiritual life and of the Great Work.

In order to be able to give, man must have, and to have he must receive, thus establishing a self-sustaining cycle between these two polarities. Through worship, expressed mainly through Prayer, man must travel inwards and upwards towards the levels of the superconscious wherein dwells the Divine Spark. He must slowly and gradually climb the Sacred Mountain at the top of which the Spiritual Self will manifest Itself and bestow upon the human self Light and Fire (knowledge, love, and life). Then through service to others expressed mainly through work and altruistic love, man must use and share what he has received from the Divine Spark . . . for unless he does so, the Light and Fire *will cease to flow* and to manifest themselves.

Introverts generally turn first towards the Spirit within and then toward their fellow-men, thereby learning how to love men through their love for God, while extroverts generally turn first toward their fellow-men, learning to love God through their love for man.

Without renewing himself on the Holy Mountain through the spiritual Light and Fire, man would grow tired and stale, and would not have anything truly valuable to offer his fellow-men. Without using and sharing what he has received from his Divine Spark with his fellow-men, the disciple would soon lose his inspiration and cease to receive more from within. Hence, both polarities are equally important and complement each other. *Prayer cannot truly function without work nor work without prayer.*

Turning to the framework of psychosynthesis, we find the same principle of Duality expressed in different terms. The two fundamental aims of psychosynthesis are first self-actualization and then Self-realization. The love of God must be balanced by the love of man, worship by service, and prayer by work.

When it comes to the mysteries of the Trinity, these are many and are ultimately unfathomable as they expand and widen with the growth of human consciousness and new levels of emergence.

One of the most basic and practical applications of these mysteries, which is explicitly alluded to by this injunction, is that of dealing with FAITH and with the effective worship of God.

Faith, spiritually speaking, is both a spiritual gift and the fruit of human labor; it is the focused convergence of *concentration, love,* and *will* upon one central point. Thus the three royal faculties of the human psyche: knowing, loving, and willing must bring their gifts (human knowledge, human love, and human creative energy) that these may be amplified and spiritualized by the Divine Light and Fire of the Spiritual Self.

Effective worship therefore entails focusing all of one's love ("all thy heart") all of one's attention or concentration ("all thy soul") and all of one's knowledge ("all thy mind") upon each word, symbol, and gesture of the Ritual which is offered to the Spiritual Self as a "vehicle of expression" to bring life to the Ritual and to connect it with the "spirit behind the letter."

Love and concentration are faculties which one acquires

through life's experiences by *using them*. Knowledge, in this case, is acquired by repeated meditation (male polarity) and by contemplation (female polarity) on the given symbol and ritual.

To truly love the Divine—both within oneself and in the world—and to love one's fellow-men as oneself is to live the spiritual life. This is what we have come on Earth to learn and to do gradually and on ever-expanding levels of consciousness and being. To truly love God means to become one with Him and to truly love our fellow-man, likewise means to become properly related to them.

Thus this injunction leads by degree to the return of the Many to the One.

This *interiorization* (climbing the Holy Mountain to receive Grace: Light, Fire, and Life) and *exteriorization* (working and sharing with others) prayer and work, receiving and giving, generates a self-starting and self-perpetuating cycle; the one activating the other and dynamizing both in the process. This is the "living" of the greatest of all Commandments, or, at least as much as can be said about it in human words!

Chapter Twelve

CONCLUSION: THE NATURE
AND USE OF RITUAL

Next to the introduction and the present conclusion, the core of this book is made up of 12 basic lectures which I have given, at first separately as autonomous units and then as an integrated seminar over a period of about seven years. Many topics and subjects have been touched upon, basically from the perspective of the Spiritual Tradition, dealing with the nature and purpose of man, with the meaning of the universe and of life, with the nature of and man's relationship to God, with the Great Work, spirituality and the unfoldment of spiritual consciousness, and, particularly, with the nature and use of Ritual as this is applied to the great "Seven Fundamentals" of the Christian tradition.

This work formed the central core of my deepest interests and aspirations for a period of about 20 years. During that time, many hours were spent reading, meditating, praying, travelling, and discussing these questions with other people who were both more and less qualified than myself. What I was after was, on the one hand, to provide satisfying answers to the deepest questions that were ever formulated within my consciousness and to find a practical and effective "art of living" that would enable me to develop the highest and best in myself, so that I could make my greatest contributions to others, and, in the process, live the most constructive, creative, and fufilling life. On the other hand, I was also after a simple and practical system that would offer direct, practical, and satisfying answers to what I feel are the fundamental questions and quests of our age, at least for some "kindred souls."

To get to the point of where I am now, and to formulate the key lectures of this book, I experimented widely with many different approaches, ranging from the psychological to the spiritual via various so-called "esoteric" and "occult" systems. I studied the teachings of different religions, esoteric schools and orders, and explored the various approaches of humanistic and transpersonal psychology. By and large, I found that every religion, school or approach did offer something, that it did contain one or two rays of that "ineffable Light and Truth" I was seeking, but that none could offer the whole or, rather, the "ready-made system" I could apply to my own unique being and life. Thus, after much reflection and experimentation, I gleaned the best I could find from these many different traditions and came up with the approach that is outlined in this book. In formulating this approach, I was guided by three major criteria:

a. The esoteric language, the great complexities and intricacies of different systems must be made simple and readily comprehensible to a sincere and mature person.

b. This approach must be practical, that is, it must be capable of being lived incarnated in one's life and being in the existing sociocultural conditions of the modern world and in the unique situation of each interested person, and it must yield tangible and constructive fruits or changes.

c. It must go to the "essence of things," touch and incorporate what is most important or go to the "heart of the spiritual quest."

d. Last but not least, it must be safe and lead one to greater psychological health and integration, and to a more productive and satisfying everyday life; it must enable one to have a fuller and richer social, personal, and professional life, and not make one a recluse, an eccentric character, or a person engrossed in his own self and particular interest and exercises.

While neither religion nor the best of the human sciences, nor even the various esoteric schools and orders I came in contact with provided a ready-made answer and system; a combination and synthesis of all of these produced the approach I am offering in this book. This approach is far from being a "system" or another "school," for it is not finished and requires much work, development, and further refinements and additions. Yet, I do believe that it can provide a sincere and mature seeker with some of the essential keys, sources, and exercises to "launch him on his way" and to enable him to find his own distinctive development and synthesis. All I can vouch for is that it has proven highly creative and rewarding in my own life and in the lives of many students who have worked and experimented with the principles and guidelines provided by this approach, and I am still working with it, ever refining it, and discovering new meanings, correspondences, and applications for it.

The central points that were discussed in this work are:

1. That we are now living in an age in which a major intellectual and cultural revolution is taking place, leading to an integral vision of reality that is grounded in a trinitarian view of knowledge, man, and the world as being physical, psychic, and spiritual.

2. That the truly fundamental problems and questions of our age, as perhaps those of any age in human history, cannot be satisfactorily answered from the perspective of either sensory, affective, or intellectual

consciousness (i.e. that science, philosophy, and religion, in their present state, cannot, by their very level of approach and interpretation, provide these answers) but only from the perspective of a higher and qualitatively different state of consciousness which has traditionally been called "spiritual consciousness."

3. That this being so, the systematic transformation, expansion, deepening and heightening of human consciousness, leading to spiritual consciousness, is now the foremost prerequisite for man and humanity to take their next step in evolution.

4. That this transformation—expansion, deepening, and heightening—of human consciousness must be a conscious endeavor which involves all the functions of the psyche as well as higher energies and inspiration than those which can be provided by the personality of a human being as it is now structured.

5. That the knowledge, the effective means, and the proper motivation necessary to bring about the dawning of spiritual consciousness can best be distilled from a creative amalgamation and synthesis of the best of the modern human sciences with the best of the sacred traditions.

6. That this new and qualitatively different state of consciousness is the product of both a new way of life, traditionally called "living the Life" and of "Prayer" as interpreted in its technical sense.

7. That Prayer, as defined by the sacred traditions, implies both a female and a male aspect; the first being known as "Entering the Silence" or consciously heightening one's sensitivity and receptivity, while the second being known as "Ritual" or consciously heightening the flow of psychic energies (the Light, Fire, and Life of the spiritual Self) flowing through

our field of consciousness.

8. That the development of spiritual consciousness involves the double quest for God and for His Church, the discovery of the spiritual Self and the development and coordination of the personality system to enable the attributes of the former to manifest in the world through the latter, and which modern humanistic psychology calls self-actualization and Self-realization.

9. That the knowledge and training of the will provided by the Occult and Magical Traditions must be balanced and directed by the unfoldment of love and faith provided by the religious and mystical approaches.

10. That the ultimate core and substance of consciousness-expansion and spiritual development is the love of God and the love of man—THE LOVE OF LIFE. All other approaches are but indirect means to that end.

11. That true spiritual work and the dawning of spiritual consciousness, or the breakthrough of the superconscious into conscious, involves both a male, or psychological part, which depends on the student, and a female, or spiritual part, which is a free gift of the spiritual Self and which lies outside the province of the will of the student.

12. That the Great Work is, ultimately, what all human beings have come to achieve on earth, and what they are consciously or unconsciously pursuing.

Within this general framework, we have seen that all religions have three fundamental parts: a body, a soul, and a spirit, and that it is the "soul" of religion which is presently "sick," and which must be furnished with a new explanation and interpretation which is congruent with the needs, ideals, and experiences of people living in today's world. We have also seen that all religions come from the same source and have the same basic goal: to lead human beings to a conscious union with the Divine. As there is one God, one basic Reality, and one common trunk for all external religions, their basic essentials are the same. In the Western Spiritual Tradition, we have identified this central core with the "Seven Fundamentals" which have their functional equivalents in all other great religions and which, when properly understood and applied, will lead any human being to his spiritual Initiation or Illumination.

We have looked at these Seven Fundamentals as including all the knowledge, the training, and the key exercises which are needed to have an integrated and effective curriculum in spiritual development. These Fundamentals were then shown to provide a training ground for all the key functions of the psyche and their major processes, namely for training:

a. The will through concentration and affirmation.
b. Thinking through meditation.
c. Feeling through adoration and devotion.
d. Imagination through visualization and, later, visions.
e. Intuition through aspiration and inspiration, invocation and evocation.
f. Sensations through observation and sensory awareness.
g. Biopsychic drives and impulses through self-mastery and transmutation.

These fundamentals were also shown as providing an ideal training ground for concentration, meditation, contemplation, and theurgy or invocation-evocation. To be sure, these basic aspects of the spiritual life can also be developed with other materials, images, and blue-prints but, those provided by the seven fundamentals are both very rich and fruitful, safe and time-proven, and integrated within the religious life of most people (with their functional equivalents in other religions) and thus they furnish an excellent starting point. The practical outline that was suggested was to take each of the Fundamentals, to identify its key symbols, petitions, and affirmations, and to use these singly, as a group, or as a whole to:

    a. Develop concentration.

    b. Practice meditation and decipher their inner meanings, associations, correspondences, and applications.

    c. Practice contemplation and get at their very heart and substance.

    d. Practice Theurgy and fill one's field of consciousness with higher Energies and Inspiration.

    e. Construct practical thoughtforms to then slowly develop, concretize, and incarnate them in one's being and life.

The standard procedure here would be for someone who has become dissatisfied with what he is and with his present life, and who is aspiring to become more than what he is—to transcend himself and to have a life more abundant—to take one of the fundamentals and to work with it for a certain period of time, ranging from a minimum of one week to a maximum of one year for each one; to carefully train his psychological functions with it, to slowly decipher and expand its meanings, associations, correspondences, and applications, and to use it theurgically as a whole to awaken the intuitive flow and a higher state of consciousness. Then, he should carefully record in a journal, or workbook, the results that have been obtained. The same can then be done with all the other Fundamentals, or with any basic document of any sacred tradition. Each year, the same procedure can be repeated so that all Fundamentals are gone through again and that one can note how much progress has, indeed, been made during the year, and how much one's consciousness and intuitive grasp have, in fact, developed.

The fundamentals can be used, in their various work phases, either alone or with a group of like-minded and interested people, and in one's Church during the regular Sunday services or shortly thereafter. Their treasures and depth are practically inexhaustible and ever-expanding with the growth of one's consciousness. The subjects they deal with and the powers and forces they work with are not only time-proven and greatly energized in the psychic atmosphere of a Western nation, but they are also safe from the many subjects and areas that could be dangerous for the sanity, mental balance, and personality integration of an average person who becomes interested in self-development and in the spiritual life.

Before true spiritual training and work can be started, a minimum of self-knowledge, self-mastery, and self-integration are a *sine qua non.* Here, I cannot recommend too strongly that interested students undergo some form of humanistic therapy (Jungian, Gestalt, or Psychosynthesis) to achieve this preliminary phase. The traditions of well-established and authentic Esoteric Orders or the guidance of a wise and loving person are also invaluable and to be greatly recommended. While it is possible for some people to do this work alone and to achieve the great prize of spiritual Illumination, it is much safer and more practical for most people to follow the other route with objective checks and the guidance of other, more advanced people.

I would be very interested in hearing from individuals or groups who plan to work on a serious basis with the Fundamentals as I have outlined them. Thus, I invite them to contact me through my publisher so that we can have some feed-back: that I may learn about the results they are obtaining by following this method and that I may inform them of further developments and experiments that I may be involved with at the time.

This book is but the beginning of a very long and exciting adventure; there will be further books and, hopefully, some form of contact will be established between interested readers and seekers, the groups I will organize, and the work I will be doing. May the Spirit grant that we meet and join efforts, and may He inspire us all for the accomplishment of the Great Work!

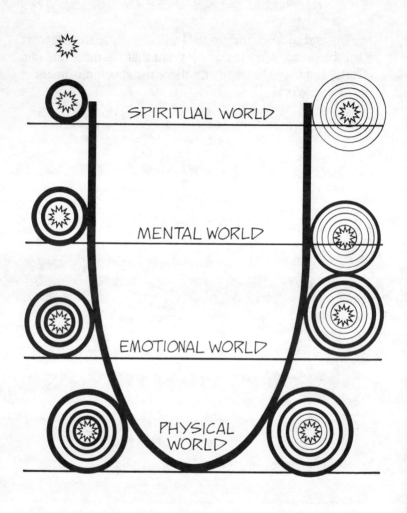

SPIRITUAL WORLD

MENTAL WORLD

EMOTIONAL WORLD

PHYSICAL
WORLD

THE FALL AND REDEMPTION

Appendix A

THE HUMAN PSYCHE
Its Nature and Structure: its Functions,
their Development and Use

In the turbulent, bewildering, and fascinating era we are now living in which is, indeed, a transitional period in which an old world is dying and a new world is being born, a fundamental consensus is slowly emerging amongst students of the human and social sciences as well as amongst students of the psychic and spiritual disciplines. This cognitive and crystallizing consensus asserts, briefly, that:

    a. Of all knowledge open to a human being, *self-knowledge* is both the most important and the indispensable prerequisite to acquire any other kind of systematic knowledge.

    b. Of all mastery open to a human being, *self-mastery* is both the most important and the logical starting point lest a veritable box of pandora be open with every new form of energy and control that man acquires.

    c. Of all quests open to a human being, the quest for *self-actualization* and the quest for *self-realization* are the most important ones which should also precede the other manifold quests that the human adventure makes available.

At the foundation of self-knowledge, self-mastery, self-actualization and Self-realization and at their very core stands a *proper understanding of the human psyche,* its nature and structures; its functions and their dynamics, unfoldment, and manifestation. It is a systematic exploration, analysis, and description of these that will constitute the subject matter of the present essay.

Another area of general consensus which is also slowly emerging and crystallizing today amongst concerned and mature thinkers is that the history of man is really *the biography of the unfoldment and expression of human consciousness;* and that the *existential essence* of man is his *human consciousness* and not his biological organism or his Divine Spark. Finally, it is also more and more agreed upon by avant-garde thinkers that it is upon human consciousness and its quantitative and qualitative expansion and transformation that the thrust of the evolutionary forces is focused upon.

One of the most important and perennial questions that human beings have always asked and answered in different ways is: What is human consciousness and its matrix, the human psyche? The term "psyche" is the Greek word which is now generally used by the human and social sciences to designate what used to be called the "soul" of man's human nature. It is the "matrix," the seat or structures, through which human consciousness emerges, flows, and manifests itself. The psyche is thus the "house," the "temple," or the composite vehicle of human consciousness. The sacred traditions generally subdivided it into the *animal, human,* and *spiritual* soul, body, or consciousness, which is made up of what the Ancients called the Four elements (Earth, Water, Air, and Fire) and that modern mystics and spiritual scientists call the *etheric, astral, mental,* and *spiritual* "body." As these cannot be seen by the naked eye or through a microscope (though they can be seen by clairvoyant sight and now seen through special screens and even photographed by the Kirlian method), they have not yet been studied by the human and social sciences which have, most of the time, denied their existence.

Since the second half of the 19th century, however, a number of independent and mystically or occultly oriented thinkers such as Helena Blavatsky, Rudolph Steiner, Max Heindel, George Plummer, George Gurdjieff, and others have again become vitally concerned with the question of the existence, the nature, and the manifestations of the human soul and have formulated unusual philosophies and methodologies to integrate the body of their studies and conclusions. A few great academicians such as Henri Bergson, Pitirim Sorokin, and Pierre Teilhard de Chardin have travelled along the same tracks and have come up with, basically, the

The structure of the psyche

Basic model: Advanced model:

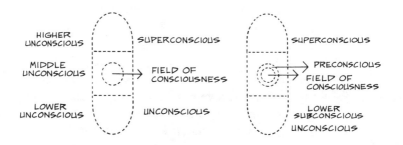

same assumptions and conclusions. In the last three decades several humanistic and transpersonal psychologists have also become fascinated with the question of the human soul and its higher reaches and potentialities. Beginning with William James and Jung and continuing with Maslow and Assagioli, new models of the psyche, its nature, structures, and functions have been proposed. With the "rediscovery" and renewed emphasis upon the will, the superconscious, the inner spaces and latent energies of the psyche, and the transpersonal energies, the following model has finally crystallized, constituting the lastest and most sophisticated model of the psyche we have up to now.

Where the basic terms are defined as:

Superconscious: those levels and energies of human consciousness lying above the threshold of consciousness and deriving their being from the Spiritual Self. It is the seat and the source of intuitions, inspirations of a lofty religious, artistic, philosophic, or scientific nature, the creations of genius, sainthood, and heroism.

Higher Subconscious: those levels and energies of human consciousness that stand between and filter the materials between the Superconscious and the conscious.

Preconscious: those levels of human consciousness that stand on the very threshold of the conscious but which have not yet penetrated into its field.

Field of Consciousness: the stream of awareness made up of the "seven functions" which manifest through speaking and acting and which derive their energies from the human self.

Lower Subconscious: those levels and energies of human consciousness that stand and filter the materials between the conscious and the unconscious. Materials which have been forgotten and repressed and which are gathered from the entire range of human experience.

Unconscious: those levels and energies of human consciousness lying below the threshold of consciousness which derive their being from the biopsychic organism of man. The psychic energies that govern the organic life of the body: the seat of the basic instincts and drives such as sexuality, self-preservation, and aggressiveness. Here are also found complexes having strong emotional charges that are produced by traumas, psychic conflict, and very painful and threatening experiences.

Simply put, these various areas of the psyche represent the consciousness of the Spiritual Self (the Superconscious) which have not yet been brought into the field of consciousness and which theology called the personal "heaven"; the consciousness of the psyche, or human self, (the subconscious, preconscious, and field of consciousness) which are partially within and partially without the field of consciousness and which theology called "purgatory" and "earth" respectively; and the consciousness of the biopsychic organism which lies outside the field of consciousness and which theology called "hell." Three major branches of contemporary psychology are now dealing specifically with each of these areas of "consciousness"; these are: psychoanalysis, or depth psychology, which focuses on the unconscious, existential psychology which focuses on the conscious, pre-conscious, and subconscious, and finally "height" or transpersonal psychology which focuses on the superconscious. The conscious, however, can be systematically expanded into the unconscious and materials and energies coming from the unconscious, the subconscious, and the superconscious can find entry into the field of consciousness thus realizing *within* man the central injunction of science: from the known to the unknown.

The Functions of the Psyche

The psyche   **The functions of the psyche:**

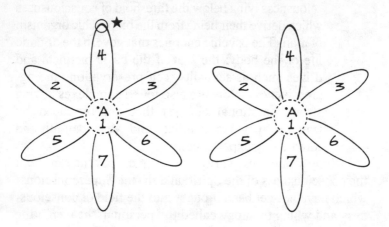

The basic terms are defined as:

★: *The Spiritual Self,* the Divine Spark, the ontological essence of man.

A: *The human self,* the conscious ego directing the seven functions of the psyche.

1: *The will,* the focused energies of the human self which activate and propel all the other functions.

2: *Thinking,* the mental process by which one grasps and makes sense of reality and of one's experiences in the world.

3: *Feeling,* energies issuing from the human self which impinge upon the field of consciousness and elicit a response. Example: joy, sorrow, surprise, awe, fear, excitement, etc.

4: *Intuition,* "seeing from within" or the "teaching from within," the spiritual function of the psyche through which a breakthrough of the superconscious takes place into the conscious.

5: *Imagination,* the image-making function which can reproduce any of the other functions within the field of consciousness and which is synthetic in nature. It has a receptive or female polarity and a creative or male polarity.

6: *Biopsychic drives, impulses-desires,* the basic drives of the body, such as hunger, thirst, fatigue, and of repressed instincts and painful experiences.

7: *Sensations,* external stimuli impinging upon the field of consciousness and eliciting a response. Example: seeing, hearing, tasting, smelling, and touching.

The first step, in exploring and analyzing the field of consciousness, is to have a map or a set of categories with which to denote the different energies and materials that flow through the field of consciousness. This "map" is provided by the seven functions aforementioned. The second step is to be able to identify, at any given moment, the operation of these seven functions, to recognize them experientially and to distinguish one from the other. The third step is to be able to deliberately train and further develop each function by a series of specific and efficient exercises. The fourth step is to coordinate and integrate these functions around the human self. The fifth and last step consists in having the Spiritual Self express Its energies and consciousness through the human self and through each of the seven functions.

After one has achieved a good theoretical and experiential grasp of the field of consciousness, one can continue and extend the exploration and analysis to the realms of the subconscious, the unconscious and the superconscious.

To do so both productively and safely one should be very familiar with the seven functions of the psyche and have acquired a good control and coordination of them through various appropriate exercises. To provide an overall sense of timing, keep in mind that some schools dedicate one year's work for the proper exploration, analysis, development, and coordination of the field of consciousness after which another year is spent on the exploration and interpretation of the unconscious and another year yet for the exploration and interpretation of the superconscious. Thus it is only at the end of the three years' work that the truly serious and systematic work really begins!

While all seven functions are important and equally part of the psyche and of the personality, there are five of them that are especially important for the inner work, both at the psychological and at the spiritual level. These, therefore, must be understood, consciously trained, and coordinated to begin the true work on the personality and the individuality (the lower consciousness and the higher consciousness). These are:

1. *The will* which must be understood in its nature and dynamics and experienced in its manifestations, and, naturally, properly trained and developed.

2. *Thinking* which must be understood in its nature and dynamics and experienced in its manifestations, and properly developed and trained.

3. *Feeling* which must be understood in its nature and dynamics and experienced in its manifestations, and cultivated and consciously directed.

4. *Imagination* which must be understood in its nature and dynamics, in its polarity and consequences, and which must be experienced and also properly developed and cultivated.

5. *Intuition* which must be understood in its nature and dynamics, in its polarity and "trigger mechanism," and which must be experienced, cultivated, and differentiated from emotion, impulse, and instinct.

The will is harnessed and applied through the process known as *concentration* and *affirmation;* thinking is harnessed and applied through the process known as *meditation* with its various stages; feeling is harnessed and applied through the process known as *devotion* and *adoration;* imagination is harnessed and applied through the process known as *visualization* and its various steps and degrees; and finally intuition is "triggered" and turned on through the process known as *invocation* and *evocation* which bring about a genuine breakthrough of the superconscious into the conscious, which opens up various "doors" and "layers" of the psyche through which different energies and materials can flow into the field of consciousness.

The inner work of man (work on the personality and on the self rather than action in the world) is based on the systematic and developmental use of these processes on all of the levels: *psychological* (development of the personality), *psychic* (exploration and use of the latent energies of the mind as in parapsychology, psychism, or witchcraft), and *spiritual* (exploration and alignment with the will and energies of the spiritual Self). These, therefore, are the true *tools* or *instruments* that are used by the practical man, the scientist, and the artist as well as by the magician, the occultist, and the mystic though, naturally, on different levels of operation and amplification. The three highest types of human beings known and venerated by human history, the Sage, the Saint, and the Hero are actually personality types in which *thinking, feeling,* and *will* have been purified, organized, exhalted, and properly aligned with the higher energies and will of the spiritual Self.

To begin a genuine and sequential work on oneself and one's personality it is thus of paramount importance to understand, to work with, and to train these various functions. There is no substitute for this work and by-passing it or engaging in it in a haphazard or negligent fashion can be very detrimental and delusional for anyone.

Appendix B

THE INTUITION
Its Nature, Components, and Proper Development

In a previous paper, we have outlined the nature, structure, and functions of the psyche, and we have briefly discussed their tremendous importance as a foundation for genuine and systematic work on one's self and personality. In this essay we shall focus upon one of the basic functions of the psyche, the intuition, and present an in-depth exploration and analysis of its nature and operation as well as the basic procedure by which to activate it and work with it.

While all seven functions have various aspects and dimensions, including the *biopsychic one* (unconscious), the *psychological one* (conscious), and the *spiritual one* (superconscious), it is intuition that is the distinctively *spiritual function of the psyche* and, as such, perhaps the most misunderstood one and the least developed at this stage in human evolution. It is intuition which links the superconscious with the conscious and that connects the spiritual Self with the human self. It is through intuition that higher energies and materials are brought through into the field of consciousness and made available to the human self and the other functions. It is through intuition that the will, the energies, and the higher faculties of the Self and the superconscious are

201

manifested, that new "doors" are open in the psyche and new layers of consciousness activated. Intuition is thus the "language of the Spirit" and the channel established between our present center of consciousness and a much higher one of which we are not conscious as yet.

The specific "language" or "units" of intuition are symbols or archetypes with their peculiar nature, dynamics, and transpersonal quality. Just as *words* and *concepts* are the language of the conscious mind so *symbols* are the language of the Deeper mind, of the superconscious and the unconscious, and their essence are intuitions with their accompanying energies and not thoughts or feelings. Symbols are also consciousness *focalizers, transmitters,* and *transformers* with a multi-layered structure and are dynamic. To understand and work with intuition it is, therefore, imperative to understand and to be able to work with symbols.

It is very easy to confuse intuition with impulse, instincts, and emotions, and most people, in fact, do that, with tragic consequences which have veiled and degraded the true nature and function of intuition which is, in fact, quite different and coming from quite another level than the former. Etymologically speaking, intuition means to "see through" or "see from within" and it also means the "teaching from within"; to "see" the Spirit and learn from the Spirit rather than from the world, from our body, or from our personality and its human experience. Our eyes, or rather attention, can be focused, externally, upon the world, upon humanity, or upon God, and, internally, it be focused upon our biopsychic organism, our psychosocial nature, the personality, or upon the Divine Spark. Intuition is focusing our attention or "inner eye" upon the spiritual Self and upon God and establishing an inner dialogue with Him. From this we can see its tremendous importance and the necessity to train it and develop it properly.

Several thinkers, from Bergson to Assagioli through

Sorokin, see intuition as the next central faculty that humanity has to develop on its evolutionary path, and some of them go as far as saying that, unless we do develop our latent intuitive powers, we shall not be able to survive the present world-crisis and transitional epoch, let alone take our next individual and collective step in evolution. As far back as the Greeks we have the statement that: man learns first and is controlled by *physis,* nature, then he learns through and is controlled by *ethos,* society, and finally that he will learn through and be controlled by *logos,* the Divine within and without. Bergson rearticulated this position when he stated that: for many thousands of years man functioned, like the animals still do, through his *instincts* which provided him with an instinctive harmony with nature and with his biological organism; then man left nature for society where he functions through his *reason* and the laws of his society which provide a conscious but tenuous and fluctuating harmony with his personality and his sociocultural environment; finally, man will yet function through a higher principle, *intuition,* which he defined as "self-conscious instinct," "instinct" coming not from the body and nature but from the spiritual Self and God which will usher humanity into the Kingdom of God. Sorokin saw intuition as the central faculty and fountain-head through which all major discoveries and cultural creations were brought into being—as man's highest faculty. Lastly Assagioli saw intuition as the faculty which we must now consciously develop . . . or perish as an ascending and evolving species. This because, for him, only intuition can now provide the insights and the understanding that we need to understand ourselves and others, to establish right human relationships and acquire the necessary *self-knowledge* and *self-mastery* which our scientific and technological achievements (the harnessing and utilization of powerful physical energies) are now making more and more mandatory if we are to respond creatively to our present impasse and world-crisis. Finally, he also claimed that it is only through intuition that human beings will realize the principle of essential divinity within themselves and in the world, and which is now necessary for us to continue our psychological and spiritual development and to meet effectively the problems and dilemmas we are, in one way or another, all confronted with.

Briefly put, intuition implies going from a given premise to its conclusion without going through the intervening mental and logical steps and to grasp the true essence and nature of anything, be it in the world or in man. Even a little reflection will show how it is this ability that human beings now need so desperately as they waddle through great inner and outer confusion, tensions, and conflicts. There is hardly a problem on which intuition cannot shed a most needed light; in fact, there are inner and outer, individual and collective problems and dilemmas that only intuition can solve at this point when our energy sources are being rapidly depleted and when another world war would wipe out life on this planet. In fact, the fundamental questions that have always existed for humanity and that each generation and each culture have had to provide tentative answers to—*the riddle of the Sphinx:* who am I, where do I come from, where am I going, what am I doing here on earth, and how can I live the most constructive and creative life; *the enigma of the universe,* why is there a universe and what is its purpose? What is man's purpose in the universe?; and *the puzzle of life,* what is life, where does it come from, what is its destiny, and how can I achieve a more conscious and abundant life—can, at the present moment, be answered satisfactorily only from the standpoint of an active and creative intuition.

While intuition is not, in its true nature and essence, a *psychological faculty* but rather a *spiritual faculty* with a different origin, structure, and manifestation, it does require the proper use of the four major *psychological faculties:*

willing, thinking, feeling, and imagination and the proper development and use of their major processess: concentration, meditation, prayer, and visualization.

Their combined and properly coordinated use yields what has been called aspiration which is used through the process of invocation, and which constitutes the *male polarity of intuition,* the human effort or Promethean thrust pointing upwards. To this male polarity, or conscious elevation and ascent of the center of consciousness, corresponds a *female polarity of intuition,* or inspiration manifesting through the process of evocation, which is the answer of the spiritual Self to the longings and askings of the human self, the Divine Grace or Epimethean response, which descends and reveals itself in the center of consciousness. Diagrammatically represented, we have the following schema:

INTUITION

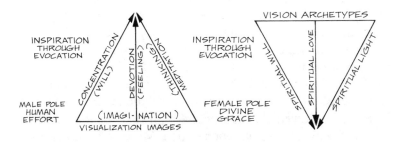

Thus to establish an active and creative intuitive flow or to activate the energies and manifestations of the intuition, we must focus all of our trained human will, and concentration, upon the spiritual Self, and all of our thinking, meditation, upon the spiritual Self; all of our feeling, prayer, upon the spiritual Self, and finally all our imagination, visualization, upon the spiritual Self. The "answer" or revelation will then come in the form of a *vision* (transforming our imagination), of *spiritual will* (revealing the will of the Divine Spark and energizing our human will to carry it out), of *spiritual love* (transforming and exhalting our human feelings and desires), and of *contemplation* (revealing to our consciousness the "Mysteries of the Kingdom," manifesting the spiritual truths and laws of our being and of the world). To *aspiration* thus corresponds *inspiration* and *invocation* is followed by *evocation,* and, in the process, a channel or bridge is established between the spiritual Self and the human self through which many energies, materials and illuminations will flow.

True prayer, in its female aspect of *entering the silence* or heightening sensibility and receptivity and in its male aspect of *ritual* or heightening the psychic voltage and energies available to the human self and the functions of the psyche, is designed to do exactly the same thing even though it uses a different terminology and approach, for the great truths and principles are the same for all ages, cultures, and human beings.

Unless man does his own distinctive work and part in the whole process, no answer and revelation will come for the Spiritual Powers do not promote "spiritual laziness" and do need human, conscious cooperation. Moreover, the spiritual energies cannot operate in a psychological vacuum; they can only work with and transform, exhalt, and amplify that which is offered. Thus, the first part of the Great Work must be the human, psychological part—the proper training, under-standing, and gradual development of the will, thought, feeling, and imagination through their respective processes of concentration, meditation, devotion, and visualization.

There is simply no substitute for that work and it is a prerequisite for the spiritual work that will follow and complete the operation.

A last important question which is generally asked and which must be answered correctly is: how do I discern what is truly intuition from what might be impulse, instinct, or emotion? How do I know that what I am "seeing," "hearing," or "contacting" does in fact come from the spiritual Self and not from the body, the personality, or the world with its many agents and subtle influences? While this is far more a question of *direct personal experience* rather than of definition or intellectual analysis, the following can be said as general guidelines:

1. The true voice of intuition always speaks very softly and gently; thus one must be sensitive and receptive enough to grasp it and not have it drowned out by the sensations, stimuli, noises, and other distractions which come from our own being or from the world and which generally fill both our minds and hearts. In other words, one must have achieved a good enough level of non-identification with the body, with the emotions, with the mind, and with the outer world before genuine intuition can be received and acknowledged . . . let alone properly interpreted!

2. True intuition as the voice of the Divine Spark never *coerces* anyone to do anything whereas impulses, instincts, emotions, and influences from the personality and the world pressure and coerce us. As an old probverb puts it: God never coerces anyone but waits patiently until He is Loved, Desired, and Bid to manifest Himself but the Devil does coerce one, diminishing both awareness and true freedom of choice.

3. True intuition, coming from the Spirit makes no mistake and does not err, even though it may reveal things which we do not like and which may require of

us sacrifices that we find very painful to make at this point. Thus should erroneous or evil promptings and "revelations" come, they cannot be from the intuition but must be from some other faculty or area of our being.

4. As the spirit is not concerned with our own personal desires or welfare but with the true welfare and long-range good of humanity, intuition will generally not manifest itself for our personal benefit alone, but for the benefit of the group in which we operate.

5. True intuition always contains a bridge or connection between the *inner* and the *outer* world. Thus when it manifests we have both an inner subjective experience of well-being, a good conscience, a feeling of fullness and happiness, a true "inner peace" or harmony, which is matched by an *outer recognition,* by some people at least, even though it might generate some form of conflict at first which will later be recognized to be actually working out for the good of all concerned.

6. True intuition always manifests itself into the three great worlds of being: the superconscious world of the spirit, in terms of energies and promptings, the rational world of the personality, in terms of illumination and the highest and most exact reason, and the physical world in terms of some action or realization.

7. Should the "voice of intuition" not be recognized, or be recognized but not implemented to the best of one's abilities, it will remain silent for a while for the Divine Spark does not have "time or energies to waste" on instruments which are not ready to cooperate in the Great Work or who are too weak and disorganized to use effectively what has been freely given. The decision here is not ours but God's, i.e. it is that of the spiritual Self and not of the human self!

Appendix C

SYMBOLISM
Its Nature and Use

Symbolism is truly the "forgotten language" of our time, as Eric Fromm put it; it is a forgotten language which, however, is fast being rediscovered and, again, explored and analyzed in depth by a growing number of thinkers in different fields. A number of world-renowned authors such as Jung, Fromm, Eliade, Campbell, Assagioli and others have dedicated a large part of their writings either attempting to define symbols and explaining their dynamics or using them and showing how other traditions and peoples have used them.

Until the Enlightenment, symbols and myths made up one of the most important languages of humanity—*its sacred language.* During and after the Age of Reason until roughly WWII, this language fell in disuse and was slowly neglected and, consequently, no longer understood in its true nature and function. In the last three decades, however, it has again come to the foreground of our culture in transition and now commands more and more attention and investigation on the part of an increasing body of scientists, humanists, and writers. Today, we find again that some things can only be expressed in symbols and that some of the most ancient and deepest truths and principles were expressed in the language

209

of symbolism, analogy, and myth rather than in the descriptive and analytical language of present day science.

Actually, there have always been three languages that human beings have used regardless of their linguistic tradition and of whether they spoke English, French, or Swahili. These three languages are:

a. *The language of everyday speech* which utilizes *words* as its units which are "handles" or instruments to *convey* and *elicit thoughts* and *feelings*. A word of everyday speech is thus said to have an intensive field made up of connotations and an extensive field made up of denotations.

b. *The language of science* which utilizes *concepts* as its units which are handles or media to convey and elicit *thoughts* (denotations) alone; ideas which are supposed to have an "empirical referens," i.e. that are capable of either observation or experience.

c. *The language of poetry and religion,* of the sacred traditions, which utilize *symbols* as their units which are handles or media through which *thoughts, feelings,* and *intuitions* are conveyed and elicited.

Thus one cannot read any of these three languages in the same way without misunderstanding their true meaning and the way they are to be used. It is this kind of confusion which has created countless conflicts and misunderstandings between religion and science during the last five centuries and which has brought about the devaluation and the demise of religion in the modern world with very grave consequences for the well-being of human beings as well as for our true understanding of both man and the world, and of their creative source, the Spirit. The reason for this is very simple: on the one hand, there has been in the Western world a gradual but progressive evolution of reason with a concomitant involution of emotion, imagination, instinct, and intuition. Thus symbols, which are the language of the irrational and superrational, were interpreted more and more in a descriptive-analytical way, which is the process by which the concepts of science are interpreted, rather than in an analogical-allegorical way which is the process that should be applied to symbols. The true meaning of symbols was thus lost and the whole language degraded and neglected.

With the development of modern psychology, particularly depth and height psychology, with the rediscovery and slow exploration of the unconscious and then of the superconscious; with the anthropological and ethnological studies of alien and exotic people of the Far-East, of Africa, South America, and Polynesia; and with the surfacing again of the sacred traditions in mysticism, occultism, and magic, it was natural and inevitable that symbolism would be looked at more critically and re-explored in its depths and potentialities. In the last three decades, a certain consensus concerning the nature and functions of symbols has been slowly emerging and has now crystallized in certain basic statements and insights which are the following:

1. Symbols are the "language" and vehicles of the *irrational* and *superrational*—which are very different in their origins and nature—and not of the *rational* part of man and of the world and life.

2. Symbols are the "language" and instruments of the unconscious and the superconscious rather than of the conscious.

3. Symbols are linked with the "right part of the brain" and with the "feminine principle" rather than with the "left part of the brain" and the "masculine principle."

4. Symbols are connected with the "night-side of life" rather than with the "day-side of life" and with the "lunar" rather than with the "solar" principles.

5. In terms of the "functions of the psyche," symbols deal with the *intuition*, with *imagination*, and with

emotion rather than with *thinking, sensations,* or the *will.*

6. Symbols use the *analogical-allegorical* method rather than the *descriptive-analytical* one. This means that they have not one socially standardized and well-defined meaning, but many meanings that are both personal and transpersonal; that they are not *static* and *closed* but rather *dynamic* and *open* with ever-new emergent levels that come to the foreground as new layers and states of consciousness are activated; that they are based on the principle of *correspondence* and *homology* derived from the great classical assumption that all things in the universe are interrelated and that the microcosm (man) is a reflection of the macrocosm (the world). This assumption was succinctly put in the Hermetic axiom "As Above so Below." Thus while there are meanings and correspondences of a given symbol that are known and agreed upon; while some of its meanings are transpersonal or collective, others are purely personal and must be interpreted from within the context of their occurrence, the level of consciousness and personal experiences of the person who is working with and using it.

7. Unlike words and concepts, symbols are not "ready made"; they are a "mine" which must be mined, a seed which must be planted and allowed to grow to reveal its flowers and fruits. Symbols, in other words, demand a great deal of personal and conscious work through concentration, meditation, and contemplation, and they must be incarnated and rendered alive in the being and life of the person who uses them. Their treasures and correspondences are never exhausted but continue to grow and to amplify as human experience is acquired and consciousness is altered and expanded. Because they function as "doors" of

the psyche and as channels to connect the conscious with the unconscious and the superconscious, they can and should be used thousands of times with ever-new results and consequences.

8. Basically, symbols are used to create a bridge, a channel, or a connection between the field of consciousness and the unconscious and superconscious, between the personal and the transpersonal, between the profane and the sacred, so that the conscious and the known can expand and grow into the unconscious/superconscious and the unknown at its own speed and according to the level of readiness of the person who is using them.

9. Another interesting property of symbols is that they can both *reveal* and *veil* a certain reality or truth according to the level of consciousness and readiness of the person who is using them; and, likewise, they can both unite or synthesize different elements and levels or separate and dissociate them. For this reason, symbols have always been the "language of the sacred traditions and of the Mysteries," revealing the inner truths to the Initiates and hiding them from the profane: expressing a fundamental truth or mystery on many different levels for different types of personality and of spiritual maturity.

10. While there is a practically infinite number of correspondences and associations which can be derived from symbols and to which they can apply, there are three basic dimensions to which they are generally applied:

   a. *The historical-literal one:* the meaning and association given to the symbol by its historical connection and its literal denotation. Here what we have is the cultural "body" or embodiment of the symbol, its surface level which is still "raw" and undeveloped, waiting to be developed and deciphered.

b. *The analogical-allegorical level applied to the microcosm, to man.* Here the symbol is applied to man, to each human being, to his anatomy, physiology, or to some archetypal level of human experience. It must be developed, correlated, and properly applied to oneself and one's daily life. What is involved is *the soul* of the symbol, which may or may not lead to its *spirit,* in one of its major sets of correspondences and homologies.

c. *The analogical-ontological level applied to the macrocosm, to the world.* Here the symbol is applied to the world, the outer universe, and its anatomy, life, and unfoldment. It must also be developed, correlated, and properly applied to the world as one perceives, comprehends, and experiences it. What is involved is again the *soul* of the symbol, which may or may not lead to its *spirit,* in another major set of correspondences and homologies.

The general line of progression in working with symbols is to go from the outer, exoteric, or historical-literal level to the analogical-allegorical level as applied to the microcosm—which is the work of the Lesser Mysteries, to the analogical-ontological level—which is the work of the Greater Mysteries.

11. All symbols have a three-fold nature: a *body,* a *soul,* and a *spirit.* The body of the symbol is the symbol itself in its cultural manifestation and embodiment—a letter, figure, sign , object, or gesture which stands for other things which must be discovered and experienced. Its soul is the many interpretations and sets of correspondences which can be linked with the symbol and discovered by working with it. The spirit

of the symbol is the *energy* and *life* with which it is connected, the Spiritual Power, Being, or Process with which it is connected, and which one has to activate in oneself by identifying oneself with it.

12. All symbols also have a *form* or shape, a *color* or set of colors, and a *name*. To the form corresponds focalization and concentration, to the color, various energies, and to the name, consciousness. Thus by working with a symbol, one has to focus one's attention and will upon a specific aspect, facet, or process of oneself, of the world, or of life; one has to invoke and experience certain energies; and finally, one has to identify and evoke a certain level of consciousness which will alter and transform the level of consciousness one is normally functioning in.

13. Symbols are thus the handles or psychic media which *convey* and *elicit* the various units of human consciousness which we call *thoughts, feelings, vital energies,* and *intuitions.* They are "streams of focused awareness," bundles of energies, the lens which *direct* and *focus* our whole attention upon one aspect of Reality, whether outer or inner; they are catalysts which convey and awaken certain energies and states of consciousness in our own field of consciousness.

In short, they are the *psychospiritual means by which we invoke a certain presence, induce a certain state of consciousness, and focus our awareness, by which we recreate, in ourselves, an image, facsimile, or representation of that which is without or above us.* They are the means by which man can deliberately awaken and focus his thoughts, feelings, energies, and intuitions by an effort of the will to link his field of consciousness with something that stands *outside, below,* or *above* that field of consciousness, thus expanding it and extending it in ever-increasing synthesis.

They are, therefore, the key regulators and main switches of human consciousness and of man's inner life. It is through them that all alterations, focusing, and expansion of human consciousness takes place, for they are regulators, accumulators, and transformers of human consciousness. They enable man to temporarily connect himself, his field of consciousness, and to identify with something greater and larger than he is and thus to slowly transcend himself and actualize his latent energies, faculties, and potentialities. For it is a well known fact that the mind takes on the form of the object it beholds and that the vital energies of man will *run along the lines traced and focused upon by the mind and cathect or energize the things or areas about which man thinks.*

By way of a practical example, let us take the symbol of Christmas. At its historical-literal meaning, Christmas is the celebration of the birth of Jesus and the recalling of the main events that took place about 2,000 years ago in Bethlehem. This is the body of the symbol. One of its major sets of correspondences and meanings, or "soul," in the microcosm is the *blue-print* of every man's spiritual initiation which lies in *the future* and not in the past! Christmas here denotes the process and major events by which the spiritual Self of a human being becomes connected with his human self and is able to express and manifest Its life and attributes (Divine Wisdom, Divine Love, and Divine Creative Energies) in one's field of consciousness and in the world. Moreover, by concentrating upon, meditating on, and contemplating this composite symbol we actually help to bring about its realization in ourselves, for all thoughts have a motor element or energy which seeks to realize and objectify itself in the physical world. Thus, far from being a purely passive experience relating to a past event, it becomes a creative process in which we have to involve all of the functions and faculties of our psyche to bring about its realization in the future.

How to work with symbols is both a science and an art; it involves a certain body of knowledge which has to be applied and certain practices which must be used and experienced in one's being and life. Briefly put, the basic way in which one works with symbols is the following: three major processes are involved: *concentration,* which focuses our consciousness through the use of the will, *meditation,* which uncovers and unveils its deeper meanings and correspondences, and *theurgy* which incarnates it and realizes its spirit in our being and life. Thus, we proceed in the following way:

1. We *concentrate* our whole attention upon the symbol we are working with to the exclusion of all other realities and things—we root our thoughts, feelings, energies, and intuitions upon it.

2. Then, through *reflective meditation,* we gather and bring into consciousness all the information, associations, and experiences we have had that are connected with this symbol. Then we empty our minds and practice *receptive meditation* to see if new meanings, insights, and correspondences will flow into our field of consciousness from the subconscious mind. Finally, we alter our state of consciousness through one of several techniques and use *contemplative meditation* to discover the essence and core of the symbol through the inspiration of the superconscious mind and the revelations of the spiritual Self. Lastly, we synthesize all of the knowledge and information gathered so that we may now use it to incarnate and objectify it.

3. Finally, through *creative meditation* or *theurgy,* we seek to become, to act out, and incarnate what has

been revealed to us through the foregoing process. We imagine that we *are* that which the symbol has revealed to us, we act "as if" we were that which the symbol has revealed to us, and finally, we slowly begin to alter our attitudes and behavior in the everyday world to conform to what the symbol has revealed to us, thus assimilating and incarnating it little by little.

Seen in this light, symbols are indeed a bridge or connection between the known and the unknown, the conscious and the Deep Mind, actuality and potentiality. They provide a blue-print by which we can progressively transcend ourselves and become more than what we are. They form a graded and progressive curriculum by which the Many can become the One, by which the Profane can be linked with the Sacred, and by which the Supreme Synthesis of finding union with God, or the fusion and alignment of the human self with the Spiritual Self, can be realized—which is the true purpose and destiny of *man* here on earth. As such, symbols are indeed the "language of the sacred traditions" and the basic units through which the *inner work* can be carried out and accomplished.

Appendix D

The Tree of Life and the Psychospiritual Centers

In several chapters of this book, I have mentioned the psychospiritual Centers of man's energy and consciousness fields. These Centers, their nomenclature, nature, implications, and correspondences, constitute a very important and fascinating, albeit complex and controversial, subject matter that cannot adequately be covered in this work. To do justice to this subject, another book is the minimum that can be expected and which I already have in the planning stage for a later time. In the Western Spiritual Tradition, this subject is related mainly to the Qabalah and the Ten Sephiroth of the Tree of Life. In the East, on the other hand, it is related to the Chakras. Excellent works have been published on this topic and can be consulted by the interested reader. The ones that I am acquainted with and consider most reliable, both in theoretical and in practical terms are:

> **Dion Fortune,** *The Mystical Qabalah,* London: Ernest Benn, 1963.
>
> **Gareth Knight,** *A Practical Guide to Qabalistic Symbolism,* London: Helios Book, 1965.
>
> **Z'ev ben Shimon Halevi,** *Tree of Life,* New York: Weiser, 1973.

Z'ev ben Shimon Halevi, *Adam and the Kabbalistic Tree,* New York: Weiser, 1974.

Israel Regardie, *The Tree of Life,* New York: Weiser, 1973.

William Gray, *The Ladder of Lights,* London: Helios Book, 1968.

R.G. Torrens, *The Golden Dawn,* New York: Weiser, 1973.

C.W. Leadbeater, *The Chakras,* London: Theosophical Press, 1938.

For the practical purposes of this work, I will include a basic diagram of the Tree of Life and list the Hebrew and English names of the Centers together with their most important meanings and correspondences.

The Tree of Life

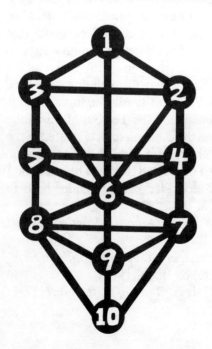

1. KETHER
2. CHOKMAH
3. BINAH
4. CHESED
5. GEBURAH
6. TIPHARETH
7. NETZACH
8. HOD
9. YESOD
10. MALKUTH

Name of the Centers	Location on Human Body	Astrological Signs
1. Kether, The Crown	Head	Primum Mobile
2. Chockmah, Wisdom	Left Cheek	Zodiac
3. Binah, Understanding	Right Cheek	Saturn
4. Chesed, Mercy	Left Shoulder	Jupiter
5. Geburah, Severity or Strength	Right Shoulder	Mars
6. Tiphareth, Beauty or Equilibrium	Heart	Sun
7. Netzach, Victory	Left Hip	Venus
8. Hod, Splendor	Right Hip	Mercury
9. Yesod, Foundation	Genitals	Moon
10. Malkuth, Kingdom	Feet	Earth

Key Correspondences
1. **Kether:** Point of contact with the Divine Spark, Unity.
2. **Chokmah:** Eternal Masculine Principle, Expansion.
3. **Binah:** Eternal Feminine Principle, Contraction.
4. **Chesed:** Principle of expanding life, Energy, Enthusiasm.
5. **Geburah:** Principle of contracting life, Order, Discipline.
6. **Tiphareth:** Intuition, Equilibrium.
7. **Netzach:** Emotion, Combination.
8. **Hod:** Thought, Separation.
9. **Yesod:** Vitality, Creativity, Conception.
10. **Malkuth:** Behavior, Resolution.

Spiritual Experience, Virtue and Vice linked with given Center
1. **Kether:** Union with God; Completion of the Great Work; none.
2. **Chokmah:** Vision of God; Devotion, none.
3. **Binah:** Vision of Sorrow; Silence; Avarice.
4. **Chesed:** Vision of Love; Obedience; Tyranny, Hypocrisy.
5. **Geburah:** Vision of Power; Courage; Cruelty.
6. **Tiphareth:** Vision of Harmony; Devotion to Great Work; Pride.
7. **Netzach:** Vision of Beauty; Unselfishness; Lust.
8. **Hod:** Vision of Splendor, Illumination; Truthfulness; Falsehood, Dishonesty.
9. **Yesod:** Vision of the Machinery of the Universe; Independence; Idleness.
10. **Malkuth:** Vision of Holy Guardian Angel; Discrimination; Inertia.

The Tree of Life with its Ten Sephiroth has its roots and being in the Four Worlds of the Qabalists. These are:

Aziluth: Divine World; Divine Consciousness.

Briah: Mental World; Superconscious.

Yetzirah: Astral World; Conscious.

Assiah: Physical World; Unconscious.

The basic task of the student of the Mysteries is to become acquainted with the Tree of Life and each of its psychospiritual Centers; to cleanse, activate, and coordinate their energies so that these can be consciously used by the Self in man's consciousness and actions.

BIBLIOGRAPHY

A. Works focusing on humanistic and transpersonal psychology.

Assagioli, Roberto: *Psychosynthesis: A Manual of Principles and Techniques.* New York: Viking Press, 1965.
_____ :*The Act of Will.* New York: Viking Press, 1973.
Dabrowski, Granger, et al (Editors): *Psychotherapies Actuelles,* Editions Saint-Yves Inc. Sainte-Foy, Que, 1977.
Harding, Esther M.: *Psychic Energy: Its Sources and its Transformations.* Princeton: Bollingen Paperback, 1973.
James, William W.: *Psychology: Briefer Course.* New York: Collier Books, 1962.
_____ :*The Varieties of Religious Experience.* New York: Modern Library, 1942.
Keyes, Ken.: *Handbook to Higher Consciousness.* Berkley, CA, Living Love Center, 1974.
Lewis, Dennis: *On the Way to Self-Knowledge.* New York: Alfred Knopf, 1976.
Maslow, Abraham H.: *Personality and Motivation.* New York: Harper & Row, 1954.
_____ :*Towards a Psychology of Being.* New York: Van Nostrand, 1968.
_____ :*The Farther Reaches of Human Nature.* New York: Viking press, 1971.

Ornstein, Robert E.: *The Nature of Human Consciousness.* New York: W.H. Freeman, 1973.

_____ : *The Psychology of Consciousness.* New York: W.H. Freeman, 1972.

_____ : *On the Psychology of Meditation.* New York: Viking Press, 1971.

Progoff, Ira: *The Death and Rebirth of Psychology.* New York: Julian Press, 1956.

_____ :*Depth Psychology and Modern Man.* New York: McGraw Hill, 1959.

_____ :*The Symbolic and the Real.* New York: Julian Press, 1963.

De Ropp, Robert S.: *The Master Game.* New York: Delta Book, 1966.

Singer, June:*The Boundaries of the Soul.* New York: Doubleday, 1973.

_____ : *Androgyny: Towards a New Theory of Sexuality.* New York: Doubleday, 1976.

Tart, Charles (Editor): *Altered States of Consciousness.* New York: Doubleday, 1972.

Wilson, Colin: *The Occult: A History.* New York, Random House, 1971.

_____ :*New Pathways in Psychology.* New York: Toplinger, 1972.

B. Works dealing with a synthesis of modern social science and esoteric, spiritual view-points.

Assagioli, Roberto: *Martha and Mary.* Kent, G.B.: Sundial House, 1975.

Bucke, Richard M.: *Cosmic Consciousness.* New York: Dutton & Co., 1969.

Eascott, Michal J.: *The Silent Path.* New York, Samuel House, 1973.

_____ : *Jacob's Ladder.* Kent, G.B.: Sundial House, 1973.

Eascott, Michal J.: *Invocation: Its Fundamentals and Practice.* Kent, G.B.: Sundial House, 1973.

_____ *:Meditation and the Rhythm of the Year.* Kent, G.B.: Sundial House, 1975.

Eascott, Michal & Magor, Nancy: *The Plan and the Path.* Kent, G.B.: Sundial House, 1975.

_____ : *Entering Aquarius.* Kent, G.B.: Sundial House, 1975.

Eliade, Mircea: *The Sacred and the Profane.* New York: Harper Torchbook, 1959.

_____ : *Myths, Dreams, and Mysteries.* New York: Harper Torchbook, 1957.

_____ : *The Two and the One.* New York: Harper Torchbook, 1962.

Jones, Gladys V.: *The Flowering Tree.* La Canada, Ca.: New Age Press, 1972.

_____ : *Reincarnation, Sex and Love.* La Canada, Ca.: New Age Press, 1971.

Leshan, L.: *The Medium, the Mystic, and the Physicist.* New York: Viking Press, 1974.

Nouy, Lecomte du.: *Human Destiny.* New York: Mentor Books, 1947.

Ouspensky, P.D.: *The Psychology of Man's Possible Evolution.* Pondicherry, India: Sri Aurobindo Ashram, 1963.

Roche de Coppens, Peter: *Spiritual Man in the Modern World.* Washington: University Press of America, 1976.

Roszak, Theodore: *Unfinished Animal.* New York: Harper & Row, 1975.

Smith, Huston: *Forgotten Truth: The Primordial Tradition.* New York: Harper & Row, 1976.

Sorokin, Pitirim: *The Crisis of our Age.* New York: Dutton Paperback, 1941.

_____ : *The Ways and Power of Love.* Boston: Beacon Press, 1950.

_____ : *Altruistic Love.* New York: Kraus Reprint, 1969.

C. Works dealing with esoteric, occult, and mystical topics.

Butler, W.E.: *Magic: Its Ritual, Power, and Purpose.* New York: Weiser, 1974.

_____ :*The Magician: His Training and Work.* London: Aquarian Press, 1963.

_____ : *Apprentice to Magic.* New York: Weiser, 1974.

Crookall, Robert: *The Interpretation of Cosmic and Mystical Experiences.* London: James Clarke, 1969.

Denning, Melita & Phillips, Osborne: *The Magical Philosophy.* 5 volumes, St. Paul, MN: Llewellyn Publications, 1974.

Fortune, Dion: *The Training and Work of an Initiate.* New York: Weiser, 1976.

_____ :*Esoteric Orders and their Work.* New York: Weiser, 1976.

_____ : *The Esoteric Philosophy of Love and Marriage.* New York: Weiser, 1976.

_____ : *Applied Magic.* New York: Weiser, 1973.

_____ : *Sane Occultism.* New York: Weiser, 1973.

_____ : *The Goat Foot God.* New York: Weiser, 1971.

Gray, William: *Inner Traditions of Magic.* New York: Weiser, 1970.

_____ : *Magical Ritual Methods.* London: Helios Book, 1969.

_____ : *The Ladder of Lights.* London, Helios Book, 1968.

_____ : *A Self made by Magic.* New York: Weiser, 1976.

Halevi, Shimon Z'ev ben: *Tree of Life.* New York: Weiser, 1973.

———— :*Adam and the Kabbalistic Tree.* New York: Weiser, 1974.

Harley, Christine: *The Western Mystery Tradition.* London: Aquarian Press, 1968.

Iamblichus: *On the Mysteries.* Translated by Thomas Taylor. London: Stuart & Watkins, 1969.

Knight, Gareth: *Experience of the Inner Worlds.* London: Helios Book, 1975.

———— :*The Occult.* London: Kahn & Averill, 1975.

———— : *A Practical Guide to Qabalistic Symbolism.* 2 volumes. London: Helios Book, 1965.

Regardie, Israel: *The Tree of Life.* New York: Weiser, 1973.

———— :*Twelve Steps to Spiritual Enlightenment.* New York: Weiser, 1973.

———— : *The Middle Pillar.* St. Paul, MN: Llewellyn Publications, 1973.

———— : *The Art of True Healing.* London: Helios Book, 1970.

Sadhu, Mouni: *Concentration.* Hollywood, Ca: Wilshire Book, 1973.

——— : *Meditation.* London: George Allen & Unwin, 1969.

——— : *Theurgy.* London: George Allen & Unwin, 1965.

Sadhu, Mouni: *Ways to Self-Realization.* New York: The Julian Press, 1962.

Steiner, Rudolph: *Knowledge of the Higher Worlds and its Attainment.* New York: Anthroposophic Press, 1968.

———— : *The Evolution of Consciousness.* New York: Anthroposophic Press, 1966.

———— : *The Stages of Higher Knowledge.* New York: Anthroposophic Press, 1969.

———— : *Education and Modern Spiritual Life.* New York: Anthroposophic Press, 1968.

D. Works dealing with a mystical and spiritual view-point.

Bailey, Alice A: *The Soul and its Mechanism.* London: Lucis Press, 1971.

_____ : *A Treatise on White Magic.* London: Lucis Press, 1971.

_____ : *From Intellect to Intuition.* London: Lucis Press, 1971.

_____ : *Education in the New Age.* London: Lucis Press, 1971.

_____ : *Esoteric Psychology.* 5 volumes. London: Lucis Press, 1971.

Bergson, Henri: *l'Evolution Creatrice.* Paris: Felix Alcan, 1930.

_____ : *L'Energie Spirituelle.* Paris: Felix Alcan, 1928.

_____ : *Les Deux Sources de la Morale et de la Religion.* Paris: Felix Alcan, 1932.

Carrel, Alexis: *L'Homme cet Inconnu.* Paris: Librairie Plon, 1935.

_____ : *La Priere.* Paris: Librairie Plon, 1944.

Chardin, Pierre Teilhard de: *The Phenomenon of Man.* New York: Harper Torchbook, 1964.

_____ : *The Future of Man.* New York: Harper Torchbook, 1964.

Charidon, Igumen: *The Art of Prayer, an Orthodox Anthology.* Translated by E. Kadloubousky and E. Palmer. London: Faber & Faber, 1966.

Echartshausen, Karl von: *The Cloud Upon the Sanctuary.* New York: SRIA 321 West 101st Street, 1952.

Heindel, Max: *The Rosicrucian Cosmo-Conception.* Oceanside, CA: Rosicrucian Fellowship, 1966.

Heindel, Max: *The Rosicrucian Christianity Lectures.* Oceanside, CA: Rosicrucian Fellowship, 1955.

_____ : *The Rosicrucian Mysteries.* Oceanside, CA: Rosicrucian Fellowship, 1966.

Lossky, Vladimir: *The Mystical Theology of the Eastern Church.* London: James Clarke, 1957.

Kopp, Joseph V.: *Teilhard de Chardin, a New Synthesis of Evolution.* Glenn Rock, NJ: Deus Book, Pauline Press, 1964.

Monk of the Eastern Church: *On the Invocation of the Name of Jesus.* London: The Fellowship of St. Alban and St. Sergius, 1960.

Papus: *L'Occultisme.* Paris: Robert Laffond, 1975.

_____ : *La Reincarnation.* Paris: Editions Dangles, 1968.

Plummer, George W.: *Rosicrucian Fundamentals.* New York: SRIA, 1920.

_____ : *Consciously Creating Circumstances.* New York: SRIA, 1955.

Saint-Denis, Jean de: *Technique de la Priere.* Paris: Presence Orthodoxe, 1971.

_____ : *Initiation a la Genese.* Paris: Presence Orthodoxe, 1971.

Sedir, Paul: *Initiations.* Paris: Bibliotheques des Amities Spirituelles, 1956.

_____ : *La Priere.* Paris: Bibliotheques des Amities Spirituelles, 1956.

_____ : *Les Guerisons du Christ.* Paris: Bibliotheques des Amities Spirituelles, 1953.

Sofrony, Archimandrite: *The Undistorted Image.* London: The Faith Press, 1958.

SRIA Documents, SRIA, 321 West 101st Street, New York, NY.

Underhill, Evelyn: *Mysticism.* New York: E.P. Dutton, 1919.

_____ : *Worship.* New York: Harper & Brothers, 1937.

_____ : *Practical Mysticism.* New York: E.P. Dutton, 1943.

MAGICAL STATES OF CONSICOUSNESS
by Melita Denning and Osborne Phillips

Magical States of Consciousness are dimensions of the Human Psyche giving us access to the knowledge and powers of the Great Archetypes that pertain to all existence.

These dimensions are attained as we travel the Paths of the Qabalah's Tree of Life—that "blueprint" to the structure of the Lesser Universe of the Human Psyche and to the Greater Universe in which we have our being.

Published here for the first time are not only the complete texts for these inward journeys to the Deep Unconscious Mind, but complete guidance to their application in Spiritual Growth and Initiation, Psychological Integration and "Soul Sculpture" (the secret technique by which we may shape our own character).

Here, too, are *Magical Mandalas* for each of the Path-Workings that serve as "doorways" to altered states of consciousness when used with the Path-Working narrations, and *Magical Images* of the Sephirothic Archetypes as used in invoking those powerful forces.

It's all here in these newly revealed techniques of the Western Esoteric Tradition.

0-87542-194-6, 420 pages, Illust.,soft.   **$12.95**

THE MEANING OF CHRIST FOR OUR AGE
by F. Aster Barnwell
Within the historical precepts of Christianity we find the *actual system taught by Christ* for spiritual awakening, and the message that each of us must accept personal responsibility for the way we live our lives and fulfill the Divine potential that is seeded within.

Going beyond such controversial books as *Jesus The Magician, Holy Blood, Holy Grail, The Nag Hammadi Library,* etc. to reveal not only that there ARE "secret teachings", but to bring them into a fully comprehensive and practical Method of Spiritual Attainment true to historical Christian documents and to proven Spiritual "teachings".

The full meaning of Christ for our age is that *"the Second Coming" is upon us now!*—that in truth it is a PsychoSpiritual experience called "The Arousal of Kundalini" in the East and "Enlightenment" in the West leading to the awakening of the dormant God-nature within.

0-87542-032-X, 240 pg., softcover.   **$9.95**

THE ODES OF SOLOMON–Original Christianity Revealed
by Robert Winterhalter
Practical steps to awaken to your Divine Self with the Psycho-Spiritual techniques of the first century Church and teachings of Jesus. The text is both beautiful and inspirational and the technique is both traditional and modern involving recent discoveries about the two brains and psycho-neurology.

0-87542-875-4, 240 pp., softcover.   **$9.95**

THE LLEWELLYN PRACTICAL GUIDES
by Melita Denning & Osborne Phillips

THE LLEWELLYN PRACTICAL GUIDE TO ASTRAL PROJECTION.
Yes, your consciousness can be sent forth, out-of-the-body, with full awareness and return with full memory. You can travel through time and space,
converse with non-physical entities, obtain knowledge by non-material
means, and experience higher dimensions.

> **Is there life-after-death? Are we forever shackled by Time & Space?
> The ability to go forth by means of the Astral Body, or Body of Light,
> gives the personal assurance of consciousness (and life) beyond the
> limitations of the physical body. No other answer to these ageless ques-
> tions is as meaningful as experienced reality.**

The reader is led through the essential stages for the inner growth and
development that will culminate in fully conscious projection and return. Not
only are the requisite practices set forth in step-by-step procedures, augmen-
ted with photographs and puts-you-in-the-picture" visualization aids, but the
vital reasons for undertaking them are clearly explained. Beyond this, the
great benefits from the various practices themselves are demonstrated in
renewed physical and emotional health, mental discipline, spiritual attainment, and the development of extra faculties".

Guidance is also given to the Astral World itself: what to expect, what can be
done—including the ecstatic experience of Astral Sex between two people
who project together into this higher world where true union is consummated
free of the barriers of physical bodies.

0-87542-181-4, 239 pages, 5¼ x 8, softcover   **$7.95**

SUPPLEMENTAL DEEP MIND TAPE
THE LLEWELLYN DEEP MIND TAPE FOR ASTRAL PROJECTION.
This is a tool so powerful that it is offered only for use in conjunction with
the above book. The authors of this book are adepts fully experienced in
all levels of psychic development and training, and have designed this
90-minute cassette tape to guide the student through full relaxation and
all the preparations for projection, and then—with the added dimension
of the authors personally produced electronic synthesizer patterns of
sound and music—they program the Deep Mind through the stages of
awakening, and projection of, the astral Body of Light. And then the pro-
gramming guides your safe return to normal consciousness with memory—
enabling you to bridge the worlds of Body, Mind and Spirit.

> **The Deep Mind Tape is a powerful new technique combining
> guided Mind Programming with specially created sound and
> music to evoke deep level response in the psyche and its psychic
> centres for controlled development, and induction of the OUT-
> OF-BODY EXPERIENCE.**

3-87542-201, 90-minute cassette tape.   **$9.95**

Note: If you have the book, THE LLEWELLYN PRACTICAL GUIDE TO ASTRAL PROJECTION, you may order
this DEEP MIND TAPE by sending full price, plus $1.50 postage & handling. Or, you can order both Book
AND Tape for a special price of just $15.00 Postpaid in U.S.A. ($25.00 overseas airmail).

THE LLEWELLYN PRACTICAL GUIDE TO CREATIVE VISUAL-IZATION. All things you will ever want must have their start in your mind. The average person uses very little of the full creative power that is his, potentially. It's like the power locked in the atom—it's all there, but you have to learn to release it and apply it constructively.

> **IF YOU CAN SEE IT . . . in your Mind's Eye . . . you will have it! It's true: you can have whatever you want—but there are "laws" to Mental Creation that must be followed. The power of the mind is not limited to, nor limited by, the Material World—Creative Visualization enables Man to reach beyond, into the Invisible World of Astral and Spiritual Forces.**

Some people apply this innate power without actually knowing what they are doing, and achieve great success and happiness; most people, however, use this same power, again unknowingly, INCORRECTLY, and experience bad luck, failure, or at best unfulfilled life.

This book changes that. Through an easy series of step-by-step, progressive exercises, your mind is applied to bring desire into realization! Wealth, Power, Success, Happiness . . . even Psychic Powers . . . even what we call Magickal Power and Spiritual Attainment . . . all can be yours. You can easily develop this completely natural power, and correctly apply it, for your immediate and practical benefit. Illustrated with unique, "puts-you-into-the-picture" visualization aids.

0-87542-183-0, 255 pages, 5¼ x 8, softcover.   **$7.95**

THE LLEWELLYN PRACTICAL GUIDE TO THE MAGICK OF THE TAROT. *How to Read, And Shape, Your Future.*

"To gain understanding, *and control*, of Your Life."—Can anything be more important? To gain insight into the circumstances of your life—the inner causes, the karmic needs, the hidden factors at work—and then to have the power to change your life in order to fulfill your real desires and True Will: that's what the techniques taught in this book can do.

Discover the Shadows cast ahead by Coming Events.

Yes, this is possible, because it is your DEEP MIND—that part of your psyche, normally beyond your conscious awareness, which is in touch with the World Soul and with your own Higher (and Divine) Self—that perceives the *astral shadows* of coming events and can communicate them to you through the symbols and images of the ancient and mysterious Tarot Cards.

> **Your Deep Mind has the power to shape those astral shadows—images that are causal to material events—when you learn to communicate your own desires and goals using the Tarot's powerful symbol language and the meditative and/or ritual techniques taught in this book to energize and imprint new patterns in the Astral Light.**

This book teaches you both how to read the Tarot Cards: seeing the likely outcome of the present trends and the hidden forces now at work shaping tomorrow's circumstances, and then—as never before presented to the public—how you can expand this same system to bring these causal forces under your conscious control.

> The MAGICK of the Tarot mobilizes the powerful inner resources of psyche and soul (the source of all Magick, all seemingly miraculous powers) by means of meditation, ritual, drama, dance for the attainment of your goals, including your spiritual growth.

0-87542-198-9, 252 pages, 5¼ x 8, illust., softcover.   **$7.95**

THE LLEWELLYN PRACTICAL GUIDE TO PSYCHIC SELF-DEFENSE AND WELL-BEING. Psychic Well-Being and Psychic Self-Defense are two sides of the same coin—just as physical health and resistance to disease are:

FACT: Each person (and every living thing) is surrounded bide the means to Psychic Self-Defense and to dynamic Well-Being.

This book explores the world of very real "psychic warfare" that we all are victims of:

FACT: Every person in our modern world is subjected, constantly, to psychic stress and psychological bombardment: advertising and sales promotions that play upon primitive emotions, political and religious appeals that work on feelings of insecurity and guilt, noise, threats of violence and war, news of crime and disaster, etc.

This book shows the nature of genuine psychic attacks—ranging from actual acts of black magic to bitter jealousy and hate—and the reality of psychic stress, the structure of the psyche and its inter-relationship with the physical body. It shows how each person must develop his weakened aura into a powerful defense-shield—thereby gaining both physical protection and energetic well-being that can extend to protection from physical violence, accidents . . . even ill-health.

FACT: This book can change your life! Your developed aura brings you strength, confidence, poise . . . the dynamics for success, and for communion with your Spiritual Source.

This book gives exact instructions for the fortification of the aura, specific techniques for protection, and the Rite of the First Kathisma using the PSALMS to invoke Divine Blessing. Illustrated with "puts-you-into-the-picture" drawings, and includes powerful techniques not only for your personal use but for group use.
0-87542-190-3, 277 pages, 5¼ x 8, softcover. **$7.95**

THE LLEWELLYN PRACTICAL GUIDE TO THE DEVELOPMENT OF PSYCHIC POWERS. You may not realize it, but . . . you already have the ability to use ESP, Astral Vision and Clairvoyance, Divination, Dowsing, Prophecy, Communications with Spirits, Mental Telepathy, etc. WE ALL HAVE THESE POWERS! It's simply a matter of knowing what to do, and then to exercise (as with any talent) and develop them.

Written by two of the most knowledgeable experts in the world of Magick today, this book is a complete course—teaching you, step-by-step, how to develop these powers that actually have been yours since birth. Using the techniques they teach, you will soon be able to move objects at a distance, see into the future, know the thoughts and feelings of another person, find lost objects, locate water and even people using your own no-longer latent talents.

Psychic powers are as much a natural ability as any other talent. You'll learn to play with those new skills, work with groups of friends to accomplish things you never would have believed possible before reading this book. The text shows you how to make the equipment you can use, the exercises you can do—many of them at any time, anywhere—and how to use your abilities to change your life and the lives of those close to you. Many of the exercises are presented in forms that can be adapted as games for pleasure and fun, as well as development. Illustrated throughout.
ISBN: 0-87542-191-1, 244 pages, 5¼ x 8, soft cover. **$7.95**